Few Torn Pages
from India's
Freedom Struggle

Few Torn Pages from India's Freedom Struggle

Subir Adhicary

Vitasta

Published by
Renu Kaul Verma
Vitasta Publishing Pvt Ltd
2/15, Ansari Road, Daryaganj
New Delhi – 110 002
info@vitastapublishing.com

ISBN 978-93-90961-38-2
© Subir Adhicary
First Edition 2023
MRP 395

Edited by Papri Sri Raman
Sketches by Maitrayee Majumder
Cover and layout by Somesh Kumar Mishra
Printed by Vikas Computer and Printers

**For my Grandchildren
Adrita & Advik**

And millions of my countrymen to read, pause
and think about the supreme sacrifices people
made expecting no return except for Freedom
that we all enjoy now.

Contents

Foreword   *ix*

Prologue   *xi*

Bhagat Singh's Shield Durga Bhabhi   1

The Muzaffarpur Bombing   8

The Alipore Bomb Case   18

The Rodda Arms Heist   25

Trench Fight At Balasore   36

The Chittagong Armoury Raid   47

The Verandah Battle   78

The Agnikanyas   91

The Heroic Saga Of Midnapore   102

Target Tegart The Terrible   125

The Flag Must Fly   132

Epilogue   *138*

Picture Gallery   *145*

Foreword

History is an integral sum of individual actions of the period for which it is studied. It is based on and includes the sum of history *prior to* the period under study. By the same logic, it influences the history of the period that follows. Therefore, to ignore individual or small group actions will be a great injustice to a fair history. These actions are influenced by the events and emotions of the period and are required to be added to the integral sum of actions of the period.

Study of recorded history of Indian freedom struggle sounds like citations of decorated heroes, read at an investiture ceremony. It definitely leaves out multitude of people, their actions and influences on history unaccounted for. When we decorate a person, we also acknowledge bravery and motivation of groups of people against whom the bravery was displayed. It would, therefore, be a historical cruelty to ignore influences of small actions by individuals or groups on our freedom struggle.

My friend Subir has chosen to write about few such people, who, in their own way, contributed to India's freedom movement. What he has politely termed as 'torn pages' were, in fact, pages never written. These are accounts of very highly motivated young men and women who influenced the course of history. They were so moved by the events that they could not sit idle and ignore the call of 'history to be created'.

Few Torn Pages from India's Freedom Struggle is an effort to bring to light historically unrecorded individuals and their contribution on the mosaic of our freedom struggle.

The book is not a biography or a compendium of records. It narrates the daring and valour of the young men and women through their exploits and who paved the road to freedom by their extreme sacrifice.

I recommend that everyone read the book and acknowledge the debt we owe to these bravehearts.

Major General Sheonan Singh, Vr. C. (Retd)
Nephew of Shaheed-e-Azam Sardar Bhagat Singh

Prologue

It was the year 1955, I was five years old. My father, a doctor in the Indian railways, had just been transferred to Lucknow. One morning, he took me and my brother to a school for admission. It was housed in a big old colonial bungalow with huge open spaces all around. The bungalow had an annexe with a temporary tin roof. There were four big rooms. We were taken to one of the rooms. There sat a frail woman wearing a white khadi saree and an assuring smile. She held out a hand to me. I approached her tentatively, only to be lifted by her on her lap. She lovingly asked me a few questions which I replied to. I was admitted to class preparatory in the Lucknow Montessori School.

Little did I knew then that I was sitting on the lap of a fiery revolutionary – an anathema for the British –

Durgadevi Vohra, fondly addressed by the revolutionaries as Durga Bhabhi. She was on the 'most wanted' list of the British police and had been arrested twice for her revolutionary activities. She was called, 'Agni of India' by the British. Post-independence, she started a school and had the support of all political leaders including Jawaharlal Nehru. I studied for nine years here and had the blessed opportunity to be near her.

In her later life, she was not accorded her due as befitted her and she died unsung.

I had, in my childhood, read about the daring exploits of Bengal revolutionaries in the Bengali books like *Bidrohi Bharat* by Dr Nihar Ranjan Gupta and others. I wondered about the absence of information about these martyrs and their acts in the books of history where some other people were highlighted. The Agniyug of Bengal – especially from the year 1900 to 1935 had hundreds of young men dying for their motherland but not before they committed some daring acts and shook the British empire up like never before. Martyrs like Jatindra Nath Mukherji (Bagha Jatin), Shrish Chandra Pal, Kanailal Dutta, Gopinath Saha, Surya Sen (Surjo Sen, popularly known as Masterda) and many others remain unknown to most of India as most of them were not given even a passing reference in the Indian history of the freedom struggle, for inexplicable reasons.

I had lost track of Durga Didi – as we at school called her. Hearing about her demise which the nation never knew about and the unfair treatment she received in the hands of the very countrymen for whom she and others had fought for, making huge personal sacrifices, I was left contemplating. Then I read about another fiery lady, Bina Das, who shot at the oppressive then Governor General of Bengal, Stanley Jackson. Though she missed her target by inches, it shook the Raj government. Released after India's independence, she fought with the authorities to get her degree certificate which was held back. She died at Rishikesh in 1986, where she lived in penury and anonymity in an ashram and ate with the beggars. Her body, found in a drain, lay unclaimed for days.

I started reading more about the unsung martyrs who made supreme sacrifices, mostly at the prime of their youth, treading a path of thorns with certain death breathing down their back, their personal lives shattered and ruined. All they were looking for was freedom for their beloved motherland. They shunned material comforts, underwent inhuman torture, went to the gallows smilingly, not knowing that they did it for an ungrateful nation.

I wrote a small eulogy for Durga Didi. My publishers, Vitasta publishers, urged me to write a book on her. It was difficult as not much information about her was available. I then thought of getting material on some more revolutionaries and bring their unsung sagas to the fore. I started looking for the torn pages of the history of India's freedom struggle.

I have recounted the lives of a few revolutionaries from undivided Bengal in this book as I was able to gather some details about them from past accounts in Bengali. Bengal contributed more to the armed revolution than most other provinces. Actions against the British Raj by Bengal's revolutionary youth were unprecedented, with meticulous planning, daring and surprise. During the thirties, after Gandhiji's assurance to get freedom through non-violence failed, the impatient youth force rose in armed movements, defying him.

The accounts came from various books written about seventy years ago, lending authenticity to the stories, from the writings of some of the actors of the actions and newspaper records. However, this is not a book for research. It is not to exhibit my literary prowess but about the prowess and valour of the men and women I set to write about. I have not loaded this book with records and long quotes. The book, written in a simple narrative style, aims at bringing forth the efforts of unknown young men and women, who smilingly made sacrifices without expecting any return.

I exhort other authors to take some time to delve into the lives of more such patriots from other States and give them their rightful place in the history of India's Freedom struggle by writing about their sacrifices.

I remain indebted to Renu Kaul Verma, who leads Vitasta, with her 'Dare to Bare' conviction and her team, for motivating me to write about my heroes, giving me a chance to highlight their acts.

My sincere thanks to Papri Sri Raman for her incisive editing and bearing with my style of writing.

I am inching towards 73 and there might be some age-induced inadvertent omissions. I hope my readers will appreciate the intent of the book and not the shortcomings.

I have no words to thank my friend of fifty-two years, Maj Gen (Retd) Sheonan Singh, Vir Chakra – nephew of Shaheed Bhagat Singh – who has written the foreword to this book in his inimitable style.

As Durga Didi imbibed in me and many others the seeds of patriotism and honesty, I have the first episode about her. Others are in chronological order. I leave it to the readers to decide whether the actions and the executors of them deserve a hallowed place in our history or not.

BHAGAT SINGH'S SHIELD DURGA BHABHI

A police sergeant named Taylor and his wife were shot at from a passing vehicle in Bombay on 8 October 1930. The Taylors were standing outside Lamington Road police station. It was the Bombay sea face, an important city promenade for Raj India, where Viceroys came to laud the Gateway to their India. The area was close to the Malabar Hills where the visiting Governor of the Punjab, Sir Geoffrey de Montmorency, had recently stayed. The newspapers cried that it was the first outrage of its kind in Bombay and was reminiscent of the anarchy in Bengal. The victims had had a miraculous escape and were slightly

Bhagat Singh and Durga Bhabhi on their way to Calcutta

injured. The shots were fired from a moving car and had, therefore, missed the target. The car was traced and the driver under intense questioning revealed that the assailant was one Gujarati lady dressed in male attire. The perpetrator and her accomplices were protesting against the death sentence to Bhagat Singh.

IN 1928, JOHN SAUNDERS, an Assistant Superintended of police, was killed by Bhagat Singh, Sukhdev and Rajguru, three revolutionaries from the Hindustan Socialist Republican Association (HSRA). They had mistaken Saunders for a senior official, James Scott, who had by ordering an indiscriminate lathicharge on a peaceful procession led by Lala Lajpat Rai, had caused him grievous injuries and death.

With police hot on their trail, it was felt that Bhagat Singh and the others should move out of Lahore. Bhagat Singh cut off his beard and hair and donned European attire. He was to go to Calcutta (now Kolkata) but for that, he had to take a detour via Lucknow and Kanpur to avoid suspicion. Sukhdev approached Durgawati Devi, known as Durga Bhabhi to HSRA cadre as she was the wife of Bhagwati Charan Vohra, a dedicated revolutionary from the group. Married to Vohra at the tender age of 11, she herself was a staunch freedom fighter and also a member of the HSRA. The association had Bhagat Singh, Chandra Sekhar Azad and other leading revolutionaries working secretly to overthrow the British regime.

Born in 1907, to a Gujarati family of Allahabad, Durga had lost her mother at a very young age and her father became a hermit, leaving her to be cared for by her aunt. As an activist of the HSRA, Bhagwati Charan had moved to Calcutta to coordinate with the secret parties of Bengal, leaving Durgadevi and their infant son in Lahore.

One night, Durgadevi heard a familiar knock at her door. Opening it slightly, she saw Sukhdev with a clean-shaven tall man, attired in European clothing, behind him. Durga let them in. To her great surprise, she found that the person with Sukhdev was none other than Bhagat Singh. He had dressed so to avoid recognition. Sukhdev requested Durga Bhabhi to accompany Bhagat Singh, disguised as his wife, which she readily agreed to do. Bhagat Singh was hesitant as Bhagwati Charan was not there and exposing Durga Bhabhi to danger, without his concurrence, was improper. Durga Bhabhi's father-in-law was a prosperous businessman with the title, Raibahadur. Durga Bhabhi's arrest would have made him accountable too. Durga Bhabhi was not worried about the outcome. She assured Bhagat Singh that she would come with him and handed him more than five thousand rupees her husband had given her for emergencies. In those days, this was a huge sum. To give credence to the disguise, she took her infant son along on the journey.

On the appointed day, Bhagat Singh bought two first class tickets for himself and his wife (Durga Bhabhi) for Kanpur. He also bought one inter-class ticket for Rajguru, who was disguised as a servant. Both Bhagat Singh and Rajguru carried revolvers for any untoward incident. From Kanpur they went to Lucknow. As the Bengal police were searching the direct trains from Lahore, they boarded a train for Calcutta in Lucknow. Rajguru left the train at Varanasi for a meeting with Chandra Shekhar Azad. The journey was uneventful but tense.

In Calcutta, Bhagwati Charan Vohra was surprised but pleased to see his wife undertaking such a daring journey.

Durgadevi went on helping the revolutionaries with money and used to meet Bhagat Singh and others in jail in disguise, after they were arrested, carrying letters and apprising them about the status of their revolution outside. Upon Jatin Das' demise due to 63 days of protest fast in jail, she accompanied his dead body from Lahore to Calcutta. Several warrants were issued against her, but lack of evidence saved her.

Later, Durgadevi hurled a bomb on Lord Malcom

Hailey, a British administrator in India, and was apprehended. She was imprisoned for three years. Meanwhile, her husband died while testing bombs near a river near Lahore; a bomb exploded in his hand near the river Ravi. His body was discovered by the police in a grave nearby. The bombs were to be used in a rescue plan to get Bhagat Singh out of jail.

Following her husband's death, Durgadevi hid for three weeks and thereafter left Lahore, disguised in a burqa. She remained constantly on the move till the hot pursuit subsided a little. Top revolutionary leaders like Azad were not happy as no prior permission, which was mandatory, was taken for the Hailey attack. The Taylor attack followed. Durgadevi slipped out of Bombay after this and again went into hiding. Her locations stayed untraced for long.

By 1940, exhausted by her hectic life, Durga Bhabhi settled in Lucknow after a brief stint in Ghaziabad. Meanwhile, she had taken Montessori training and had started a school, the Lucknow Montessori School, in a big bungalow near the Lucknow Publishing House, near Burlington Hotel. The sprawling school started teaching with just five students and by 1950, with the blessings of Pandit Jawaharlal Nehru and Congress stalwarts like Rafi Ahmad Kidwai, Acharya Narendra Dev, Sampoornanand, the school had more than 200 students. Pandit Nehru came every year to the school and exhorted the students to be good citizens, distributed certificates and released doves signifying peace. He mingled with the kids freely. The fact that the Prime Minister of India came visiting each year reflected the respect and stature Durgadevi commanded. In 1955-56, land was allotted to the school in Purana Quila area of Lucknow. Nehruji laid the foundation.

Durga Bhabhi was a frail little woman with an iron will and a pleasant personality. She loved children. She breathed her last in Ghaziabad in 1999, in her son Sachindra's house. Unfeted, unsung and unheard of, Durgawati Devi remained an enigma for the British police and was referred to as 'Agni of India'. She remains a legend in the context of the sacrifices and bravery exhibited by India's women striving to free the motherland from the colonial aggressor.

THE MUZAFFARPUR BOMBING

A meeting was underway in a hut adjacent to a ruined temple. A lamp flickered in the temple, lighting up the idol of Goddess Kali with her menacing looks. In that dim light the young men present there spoke in hushed tones. The leader asked whether the boys were ready to sacrifice their lives for the Motherland. A 13-year old — Khudiram bose — first raised his hand. Then, several other hands came up. The leader hugged the teenager and promised an action soon which the countrymen would remember. Thereafter, the young men melted into the liquid darkness one by one.

Prafulla Chaki and Khudiram Bose throwing bombs at a carriage

THE YEAR WAS 1902.

Midnapore in Bengal (Medinipur) was the hub of revolutionary activities aimed at overthrowing the British empire in India through armed struggle and attaining freedom. Hundreds of young men were initiated into the secret missions being planned in various small health clubs, known locally as *akharas* or *anushilan samitis,* serving as a facade for the revolution. Secret meetings were held to motivate members, and plan and coordinate the missions to terrorise Raj India.

Satyendra Basu was one of the several young men who provided leadership to such groups and the armed struggle movement. He and his brother Gyanendra led a group mobilising youth of the nearby town and neighbourhood areas. Present among them was Khudiram Bose, a 13-year old, who had come to the notice of the leaders for his commitment and daring even at that tender age. He was also a regular at the local health club and despite being a frail youth, was full of energy. Losing his mother at a tender age of six, he was lovingly raised by his elder sister.

For the next three years, the boys engaged themselves in boycotting imported material, distributing inciting pamphlets and engaging in skirmishes with the police. Once, Khudiram was distributing anti-establishment pamphlets at a fair when a policeman noticed it and caught him by collar. Khudiram landed a strong punch on the policeman's nose, sending him reeling to the ground and attempted to flee. Several other policemen ran after him, caught him and beat up Khudiram, before arresting him. Satyendra, who was close by, came running and scolded the policemen for having arrested the son of the Deputy Saheb. Flustered by Satyen's words, the policemen released Khudiram, only to realise a tad too late that they had been fooled. By that time, Khudiram and Satyen had made good their escape.

Three years later. Bipin Chandra Pal, a well-known leader, was being tried at the Chief Presidency Magistrate's court in Calcutta. The magistrate, Douglas Kingsford, was in charge of sedition cases. He was an infamous person hated by one and all for the severe punishments he meted out even for minor cases of anti-British acts. The courtroom on the date of hearing was crowded with onlookers. A 15-year old named Sushil Sen was in the crowd.

As Kingsford took his seat, the crowd jostled to get closer and listen to the proceedings. The court police, led by one Inspector Hughes, under a fit of rage, started beating people up indiscriminately and then finding the child cowering in a corner, rained blows on him. Initially taken aback, Sushil punched Hughes on his face, which infuriated Kingsford. He was livid that a 'native' had the temerity to beat an English officer in his court room. He ordered the policemen present to cane Sushil, which the police did with pleasure, beating Sushil to a near-dead condition, much to the surprise and shock of the crowd present there.

This incident sent waves of anger throughout Bengal and the revolutionary organisations planned to punish Kingsford. In one of the secret meetings, a death sentence on Kingsford was unanimously passed. Kingsford was to be eliminated by a bomb blast. The two people chosen to accomplish the task were Khudiram Bose and a young man called Prafulla Chaki, alias Dinesh. The wait was now for the right moment and place.

An opportunity presented itself soon. A few months later, Kingsford was transferred to Muzaffarpur (now in Bihar. Bengal and Bihar were one administrative unit in the 1900s) as Session's Judge. The security at that place was lighter than in Calcutta.

One morning, Khudiram met Prafulla at the Howrah station. This was their first meeting, in order to maintain secrecy. They took a train to Muzaffarpur and checked into a Dharamshala (a traveller's inn). There, Prafulla handed over a pistol and ten cartridges to Khudiram. The Calcutta police, by then, had received information about an attack on Kingsford being planned. As Khudiram and Prafulla had checked in under assumed identities, the police team that was sent to investigate went back. The boys waited in Muzaffarpur for three weeks.

30 April 2008. Eight o'clock in the evening.

The local European Club was full of merrymakers. The sound of piano drifted out along with laughter. Outside the club, under a big tree, two shadows stood like rock, their eyes shining in anticipation and excitement. They had definite news that Kingsford was there in the club and was riding his favourite fitton (also called phaeton or buggy, a horse-driven carriage). Minutes ticked; hours rolled. At last, the fitton emerged from the club gate. The eyes of the shadows glared. They ran towards the carriage and hurled the bombs. There was a huge explosion and flare. The merriment stopped and everyone ran out. The shadows ran in opposite directions, elated that they had accomplished their onerous task. Little did they know that fate had intervened. Kingsford had changed his plans at the last moment and offered a lady named Kennedy and her daughter a ride back home, while he stayed back in the club.

Entire Muzaffarpur was in turmoil as the news of the attempt to kill Kingsford and the resultant death of two English women spread like wildfire. Oblivious of this, hounded by the police, Khudiram ran to Waini station while Prafulla ran towards the Samastipur station. They were never to meet again.

Khudiram walked the whole night to reach the station. He was thirsty and approached a tea stall for a glass of water. Two policemen, looking at his exhausted appearance and dusty feet, got suspicious and confronted him. Upon questioning Khudiram, they became more suspicious, and a struggle soon ensued. The policemen, being stronger than Khudiram, held him down. One revolver fell out from Khudiram's clothing and on search, another revolver and 37 rounds of ammunition were found on his person. Khudiram was brought to Muzaffarpur where the station witnessed a near stampede when the huge crowd jostled to have a look at the young boy. *The Statesman*, on 2 May wrote:

> The Railway station was crowded to see the boy. A mere boy of 16-17 years, who looked quite determined. He came out of a first-class compartment and walked all the way to the phaeton, kept for him outside. Like a cheerful boy showing no anxiety, on taking his seat the boy cheerfully cried, *Vande Mataram*.

Khudiram took the entire responsibility of the attack until he was shown Praffula Chaki's severed head. His trial started on 21 May 1908. There were two long hearings which culminated in a death sentence – to be hanged till dead. A smiling Khudiram welcomed the sentence. Upon being asked by the judge whether he understood the meaning of the pronounced sentence, Khudiram nodded in the affirmative. When the judge asked him again whether he had something to say, Khudiram replied with the same composure that in case he was given a little more time, he could teach the judge the skill to make bombs. The exasperated judge left the chamber.

Khudiram went to the gallows on 11 August 1908, cheerfully smiling while the hood was drawn over his head. His mortal remains were taken in a huge procession. At the time of hanging, Khudiram was only 18 years and 8 months old, making him one of the youngest revolutionaries of the Indian freedom struggle.

Khudiram has found his place in the annals of history due to his hanging at the gallows at a young age which sent shock wave throughout the nation, but his partner in the daring act – Prafulla Chaki has not been given his proper due.

Prafulla was born in the year 1888 into a well-to-do landowning family in Pabna (now in Bangladesh). While he was in class nine, he was expelled from school for taking part in anti-government demonstrations. He then developed contacts with the revolutionaries in Bengal and took part in their actions. He was a good horse rider, swimmer and an accoladed wrestler. Moving to Calcutta, he joined the Jugantar party, a pro-armed revolution group. He was earlier assigned to kill the first Lieutenant Governor of East Bengal. The plan did not materialise and later, he was given the task of eliminating Kingsford, alongwith Khudiram Bose.

After the club bombing, Prafulla ran towards the Samastipur station to catch a train to Mokamah. The train was due late at night. He was given refuge till the train came by, by a kind railway staff, Triguna Ghosh, who provided him with an Inter-class ticket too. Prafulla looked ruffled and tense. Unfortunately for him, a police officer named Nandalal Banerjee was travelling in the same compartment, in plain clothes. Sensing Prafulla's troubled body language and knowing about the bombing incident, Nandalal got suspicious and began talking to him. Prafulla, under terrible mental strain, blurted out his story to the seemingly friendly man. At Mokamah, both got down and Prafulla went over to the water tap to drink water. Meanwhile, Nandalal alerted the Railway police, who encircled Prafulla from all sides. Trapped, Prafulla pulled out his own revolver and committed suicide by shooting himself in the head right there on the platform. His shattered head was gorily beheaded by the police, and sent to be identified by Khudiram, who had been by then arrested at Waini station. Thus, one more young man with a zeal to free his motherland gave his life for India's freedom. Triguna Ghosh was arrested for complicity and sentenced to jail.

Nandalal Banerjee was assassinated later by two revolutionaries Srish Chandra Pal and Ranen Banerji in broad daylight as he stepped out of his house – pleased with his promotion and reward money. Ranen hit him first, causing Nandalal to slump on the pavement, then Srish Pal emptied his pistol into Nandlal's head. The duo walked off non-chalantly before the stunned crowd could react. Chaki was avenged.

THE ALIPORE BOMB CASE

The court room resonated with cries of Vande Mataram every time the revolutionaries were brought in. There were more than thirty young men in handcuffs. All was well and a certain amount of daredevilry and merriment was in the air, every time they appeared in court until it was known one day that one of the boys, named Narendra Gosain, had turned a government approver and was ready to reveal all. There was disbelief in the prison. The news got credence when Narendra moved out of the regular cell to a secure hospital cabin in the European ward, with a guard keeping a watch over him all the time.

Kanailal shooting Narendra Gosain

RISHI AUROBINDO GHOSH, A sage settled later in Pondicherry (now Puducherry), was in his earlier years a revolutionary who ignited the minds of many young men in undivided Bengal. He was a respected leader, well read, articulate and a visionary. He was a close associate of Lokmanya Tilak. Rishi Aurobindo is a well-known and revered name in today's India.

Barin Ghosh, born in 1880, was the younger brother of Rishi Aurobindo. The Ghosh brothers came from an affluent family and Barin was born in England. The brothers were deeply involved with armed revolution and their sprawling farmhouse in Alipore, Calcutta served as a safehouse and bomb-making facility. The brothers, after a misunderstanding with a senior leader of Atmonnati club, started a new group called Jugantar (bhasha word for change of era) in 1906. It became the largest underground party in no time.

The safehouse at Alipore had many young men without money, food and basic amenities of life staying in it. Undaunted, they carried on their work to free India from colonial rule. Their leader, Barin, though a lanky figure, had dreams and determination in his large eyes and commanded respect of other group members.

Most of the bombs used in actions against the British were made in that safe house. The main bomb maker was

Ullaskar Dutta under Hemchandra Kanungo. Hemchandra had sold his house and with that money travelled to Paris where he learnt the nuances of bomb making with picric acid. On return, he taught the art to many youths.

A few days after the Kingsford murder attempt, just before dawn, the house was encircled by a huge police force. The officer-in-charge knocked at the door vigorously. The door was opened by Barin Ghosh, who identified himself. He was arrested forthwith, and the house was searched. The youths present were rounded up in the mango grove of the farmhouse. Ransacking the house and digging the lawn, the police discovered a few pistols, ammunitions and bomb-making materials.

Barin, Hemchandra, Ullaskar, Upendra, Rishikesh, Kanailal and Satyendra were arrested. Aurobindo Ghosh was picked up from his residence elsewhere. In all thirty-four people were convicted of treason.

The famous Alipore Bomb Case trials started with much vigour. The British were furious after the Kennedy murders. The case was important for them and they wanted to implicate and sentence the men involved. The men facing trial were upbeat though.

Kanailal Datta was the only son of a widow from Chandannagore, near Calcutta, then under French rule. He was also arrested under the same bomb blast case. He was just 20 years old. Furious at Narendra Gosain's treacherous act of turning approver, he joined Satyendra Bose in planning the elimination of Narendra. By then, Narendra had revealed many names of young revolutionaries, hitherto unknown to the police.

Satyendra Bose, the one who had mentored Khudiram, was upset at the failed attempt and wanted to stop Narendra from revealing more names. As he had lung disease, he got himself admitted to the same hospital. A pistol was smuggled in and given to him, but it was too heavy to be used. It was replaced by a smaller weapon. Kanailal joined the hospital later and made plans with Satyendra about killing Narendra before he did further damage to their great cause.

Kanailal also got himself a revolver. Narendra was approached by the two and over the next few days, they made friends with Narendra and told him that they also wanted to become 'approvers' and wanted to provide more information to Narendra about the group's activities. Convinced, after some days Narendra agreed to meet Satyendra and discuss the issue. Narendranath was confined in the European ward and was taken to the general ward, escorted by a Eurasian guard, where he was to meet Satyendra and Kanailal. The moment Narendra appeared at the landing of the second floor of the hospital, Satyen pulled out his revolver and fired at him. Narendra's escort jumped at Satyen and was hit in the hand. The bullets did find Narendra but were not fatal. Narendra ran with all his strength down the stairs, through an alley, towards the gate. Kanailal, like a tiger on the hunt, ran after him and shot Narendra through his back, killing him instantly.

Kanailal was held by a prison guard and pinned down. The daring act was unparalleled in the prison's history. It showed that treachery had no place in revolution.

The daredevilry, bravery and the swiftness of the action was talk of the town. Kanailal refused to appeal for clemency. He stated, 'There shall be no appeal'. The use of *shall* was in the imperative.

Asked about his motive, Kanailal said, 'I wish to state that I did kill him. I do not wish to give any statement about why I killed him. Wait, I do wish to give a reason. It was because he was a traitor to his country'.

Kanailal, convicted and sentenced to death, was hanged on 10 November 1908.

A day before his execution, a smiling Kanailal was told by an English warden that his smile would disappear from his lips the next morning.

The next morning, just before the hanging the warden met Kanailal near the gallows. Kanai was still smiling and asked the warden, how he found Kanailal's demeanour now. The warden was stunned. He later confided to one of the senior revolutionaries that if they had a hundred men like Kanailal, their aim to get freedom would be fulfilled.

The day of cremation saw an ocean of humanity jostling to get a glimpse of his face. His body was bedecked with flowers and a big procession followed.

Satyendra Bose was also convicted and sentenced to death by hanging. The commotion at Kanailal's funeral forced the police to hang and cremate Satyen within the prison premises on 21 November, 1908. He was 26 years old at the time.

The elimination of the key witness, Narendra Gosain, weakened the Alipore Bomb case severely and Aurobindo and a few others were acquitted while all the others arrested were given jail sentences.

THE RODDA ARMS HEIST

Seven bullock carts waited patiently in the early morning, in a lane in the Bowbazar locality, near the Customs House, in the heart of the city of Calcutta. In August 1914, news had come that a huge consignment of arms and ammunition was expected to arrive by a ship called 'Tactician', docking at the Calcutta harbour. The consignment was to be taken to the godowns of R B Rodda & Co, at Wellesley Place. The goods included fifty German-make Mauser pistols and fifty thousand rounds (five lakh bullets) of cartridge. This was meant to be sent allegedly to the Dalai Lama in Tibet. This was the 13th Dalai Lama, Thubten Gyatso.

Looted arms being transported to the Rodda & Co godown

IN APRIL 1930, ARMED revolution against British rule in India saw one of its most daring actions – that of looting the Chittagong Armoury under the leadership of Surya Sen (known as Masterda). An equally daring act was carried out years before that. On 26 August 1914, fifty Mauser pistols and five lakh bullets were looted from Dalhousie Square; the arms belonged to Rodda & Company. *The Statesman* newspaper described it as 'The Greatest Daylight Robbery'. A meticulously planned and audaciously executed anti-British act has faded into oblivion under wraps of a dusty history, long forgotten.

At that time, most countries in the West were engaged in World War I. Against the backdrop of this war, Rash Behari Bose, Bagha Jatin (Jatindranath Mukhopadhyay) and other revolutionaries had planned an extensive armed uprising across the country. It seemed the best time to strike when Britain was busy fighting elsewhere in the world.

At that time, there were many secret revolutionary organisations and all of them were short of arms. There seemed only two ways to get them. One was to buy from the black market at a very high rate, which was not possible due to paucity of funds that anti-government forces faced. The other option was to look to helpful rich persons for funds to buy arms. Between arms and the armed uprising was a gap so wide that, to be able to bridge this appeared to be a dream for India's zealous and impatient revolutionaries. Still, the revolutionaries did not lose heart.

The Anushilan Samiti, set up by Satish Bose, Sarala Devi and others was in the forefront of the revolutionary organisations and it had spread all over India with concentration in Calcutta and Dhaka. By 1906, an offshoot group called, Jugantar, headed by Aurobindo Ghosh, Barin Ghosh and Bhupen Datta (who was Swami Vivekananda's younger brother) was set up for accelerated action. Then there was a very active group, known as the Hemchandra group, led by Hemchandra Ghosh. At the same time, the Ghadar Party, mainly formed of Punjabi youth in the USA, had sent back to India, thousands of their activists to ally with the revolutionaries in Bengal and create rebellion in the cantonments where the British held their Indian soldiers, sending them into a war that was not India's. All these revolutionaries saw a great opportunity in the war to rock the citadel of British rule in India. However, they were all short of arms and looting British ammunition was one way of resolving this shortage.

Securing tacit concurrence from Bagha Jatin and other senior leaders, a group of young men planned a daring arms heist from the Rodda company godown in the middle of the city. The team consisted of Anukul Mukherji, Srish (Habu) Mitra, Biman Ghosh, Srish Chandra Pal and others. Habu Mitra, a daring youth of 24 years, was trained as a revolutionary by Anukul Mukherji and was employed with Rodda & Co. Due to his hard work and strong physique, he was in the good books of the Manager, Mr Pike. The manager gave Habu Mitra the duty of getting the shipments meant for the company released from the dock, which he did adroitly. It was he who had given the revolutionaries the information about the expected ammunition consignment.

The planning part was given to Srish Pal who was the most daring of them all. Hailing from Dhaka, he was operating from Calcutta posing as a fish dealer. He had earlier, in 1908, along with Ranen Ganguly, shot dead the police inspector, Nandalal Banerjee, who had betrayed Prafulla Chaki. (Prafulla Chaki and Khudiram Bose had attempted to kill magistrate Kingsford in Mujaffarpur.)

Srish Pal, after his hit at Nandalal, had gone underground and had surfaced again in 1913. The police had failed to apprehend him in the six years in between, despite intensive search operations.

The daring plan to loot the arms was made by Pal. A bullock cart, apart from the six already hired by the Rodda & Co, was to be arranged. This was to be driven by a young man called Haridas Dutta. Srish Pal and Khagen Das were to walk on both sides of this cart, with revolvers tucked in for exigencies. Four youths were given the task of lookouts for plainclothes policemen in the area. They were to sing aloud in case of any danger.

On the early morning of D-Day, Haridas was dressed as a Bihari cart puller. His makeup was done by a student from Bihar, Prabhudayal Himmatsinghka; his hair was cropped, and he was dressed in a black vest and a dirty *dhuti* (a wraparound) and wore a brass neckpiece. Apprehensions were whether Haridas would be able to drive the bullock cart but he did it splendidly and twisting the tail of the bullocks, he headed the cart towards Strand Road in Bowbazar where the Customs House was located. With a revolver tucked under the shirt, Srish Pal followed the cart. The day had started.

26 August 1914. The office area in the heart of Calcutta was busy as ever. The luggage Babu of Rodda & Co, Habu Mitra, reached the Customs House in European attire. He looked impressive. Six bullock carts had reached the place; they were waiting for the seventh one – the one Haridas Dutta was driving in disguise. Habu Mitra scolded him for the delay and feigned anger. As many as 202 wooden crates were released, of which 192 were loaded on to six carts. The seventh had the remaining ten crates.

The carts moved towards their destination, the Rodda & Co's godown, with Habu walking along the carts.

The first six took the lane towards the Rodda godown in Vancitart Row.

The seventh one, unnoticed, quietly broke away from the file and moved eastwards, followed by Khagen Das, casually walking behind and the mastermind, Srish Chandra Pal following Das, all the while their hands on their hidden revolvers.

Crossing Mango Lane, British Indian Street, Bentinck Street and Chandni Chowk, the cart came to a stop in Malanga Lane. There was a scrap yard there; the crates were unloaded here. The cart driver, Haridas Dutta, was asked to leave the area and a little later, Srish Pal and Habu Mitra who had joined him by then, left the place. Another revolutionary, Anukul Mukherji, was asked to transfer the crates to a safer place. He arranged two horse buggies, and with the help of other revolutionaries, the crates were taken to Jelepara where a sympathiser, Bhujanga Dhar, stayed. There, during the night, the fifty Mauser pistols and five lakh bullets were stuffed into boxes of different sizes.

This was the most advanced armament that the Indian revolutionaries had ever laid hands on. The German pistols could be used as rifles, simply by attaching a wooden piece to extend their length. Each bullet strip contained ten bullets, making it a round. The firing time was fast, and the range was about 500 meters. The junior group members who helped unpack, repack and clear the house were unaware that these were looted arms. Till the next evening.

Srish Pal knew that suspicion would surely fall on Habu Mitra, Rodda's employee. He took Habu to Rangpur to stay under cover at Dr Suren Bardhan's house and immediately returned to Calcutta. The looting was done in such a meticulous manner that Calcutta police had no knowledge about it till Rodda& Co filed a complaint about the missing arms, a day later.

The report about the missing arms sent a shock wave among the police force. The infamous head of the Special branch, Charles Tegart, was livid. Information soon arrived that two horse carts were seen shifting some boxes from Malanga Lane to Jelepara. The cart owners were traced, and the house of Bhujanga Dhar was raided. There was nothing there. The revolutionaries had already shifted the cache to another rented godown. The police found that godown too. Srish Pal then instructed Haridas Dutta to shift the loot again. As Haridas went to move the boxes, the godown chowkidar alerted the police and one policeman called Ali Hussain reached there and took Haridas to the police station. On the way, Haridas, on the pretext of tying his shoelaces, stooped down, picked up some dirt and threw a fistful into Hussain's eyes and ran away. He threw the godown keys into a manhole. Hussain started shouting,

'*Daku bhag raha hai* (the dacoit is running)' and as usual, the over-enthusiastic Indian public around apprehended Haridas and handed him over to the police.

Tegart himself took Haridas to the godown, broke the lock and to his utter dismay, found only about 2 lakh of bullets. The rest of the ammunition was missing – that was fifty pistols and about 3 lakh bullets.

By then, the missing arms were distributed among different revolutionary groups. The arms were distributed to most of the groups and no discrimination was made. Bagha Jatin and his accomplices got some pistols and bullets, with which they fought the Battle of Buri Balam – a great battle in the annals of the fight for India's freedom.

Habu Mitra's absence from duty after the looting pointed to his complicity and the police made out a list of his acquaintances like Anukul Mukherji, Kalidas, Bhujanga Dhar, Prabhudayal Himmatsinghka and others. Srish Pal and Khagen Das could not be apprehended. The Rodda & Co arms conspiracy case ran for seven months. However, the operation was so smooth that only a few of the accused were sentenced to two years of jail each. Only Haridas was sentenced to four years of imprisonment. These were early days for the armed revolution in India and Charles Tegart's rule.

Habu Mitra left Rangpur for Assam and trying to cross over to China with a local tribal chief, vanished for ever. He was presumed to be mauled by wild animals in 1915. His date of death is unknown. His village in the district, in the Howrah-Amta block, celebrates 26 August, the date of the heist, by unfurling the national flag even today at a small memorial there.

The mastermind of this daring heist, Srish Chandra Pal was arrested in 1916. The charges against him for murder of Nandalal Banerjee could not be proved. His complicity in the arms loot earned him life imprisonment. In 1919, he was released on medical grounds. He did not stop after release. He attempted to murder two British engineers who had killed a poor labourer. He then hid again, to resurface in 1928, and offered his and his group's services to Netaji Subhas Bose's Bengal Volunteers. He died of ill health in 1939.

Only by 1917 were the missing arms from Rodda &Co partly recovered from all over Bengal. By then, about 27 British officials were killed and about 44 injured with these pistols (on record). The pistols were distributed amongst all revolutionary groups though the heist was executed mainly by a group led by Hemchandra Ghosh. Years after independence, Anukul Mukherji's nephew Gopal Mukherji (known also as Gopal Pantha) took the initiative to install busts of Anukul Mukherji, Bipin Behari Ganguly, Gorib Banerjee and Haridas Dutta at Ganesh Chandra Avenue in Kolkata. A wooden replica of the Mauser pistol is kept there. This memorial, however, does not have the statues of the main characters like Srish Chandra Pal and Habu Mitra.

This day, 26 August, comes and goes every year. The busts remain neglected. Sometimes, local clubs clean them up and garland the young revolutionaries who fought for freedom against all odds. As there was no gunfire exchange, deaths or gallows, perhaps this story remains uncelebrated. What one forgets is the meticulous planning, extreme daring and a successful heist, giving a fillip to the fight for India's freedom.

TRENCH FIGHT AT BALASORE

Year 1906.

Some villages around Kushtia, a sub-divisional town in erstwhile undivided Bengal, were terrorised by a Royal Bengal Tiger. Fanibabu, a local man, decided to kill the tiger and set out on foot with a gun to find the beast. He was accompanied by his cousin, Jatindranath Mukherjee (27) and a few more villagers, all armed with lathis (wooden sticks). Jatin carried with him a Gurkha dagger (kukri) for added safety. Treading cautiously through the dense forest, they accosted the tiger. Fanibabu took a shot at it but missed it just by inches. Enraged, the big tiger lunged at Jatin, who was standing near Fanibabu. It bit and clawed him as he fought bravely, stabbing the tiger repeatedly with all his strength. Jatin was a body-builder and possessed enormous physical and mental strength. The fight ended when he was able to plunge his dagger deep into the tiger's neck. The tiger, exhausted and bleeding profusely, lay dead as Jatin lay over it. He was, after initial medical aid, taken to Kolkata where a top surgeon, impressed by his courage and grit, took upon himself to treat him. Jatin suffered about 300 lacerations. Jatin now fought again, this time with death, and emerged victorious. The doctor nicknamed him 'Bagha Jatin' or 'Tiger Jatin'. This nickname stuck to him lifelong.

Jatin's exploits were published in the English and vernacular papers and the Government of Bengal presented him with a silver shield with an engraving, showing him fighting the tiger.

9 SEPTEMBER 1915.

In a small hotel in the sleepy hamlet of Chasakhand in the district of Balasore, Odisha (then Orissa), five young, tired and dishevelled men were having a meal. Sometime later, a villager came in and sitting down with a cup of tea, told

Bagha Jatin and his companions fight an unequal battle

the hotel owner, with excitement written all over his face, that the village was abuzz with policemen and soldiers. On hearing this, the five young men rose from their table, paid the hotel owner, and left in haste. The villagers, suspecting them to be bandits, followed them. The five men ran through the seashore jungles and marshlands, with the police and the villagers in hot pursuit. Nearby, the river Buri Balam flowed towards the sea through an undulating terrain. Finding an improvised trench, the youths jumped into it and took up positions. They had German Mauser pistols with them. To deter their chasers, they fixed their pistols on to dry sticks, to resemble guns, if seen from afar. The higher terrain, where the trench was, gave them a vantage position for shooting.

However, in no time, they were surrounded by a crack police team, led by the infamous and the toughest Commissioner that the Bengal Police had ever had, Charles Tegart. He was joined by the District Magistrate of Balasore, one Mr Kilby and his forces, along with a British army lieutenant called Rutherford. This large contingent mounted a pincer attack on the fleeing youth, with sophisticated armaments. However, exhibiting remarkable resilience and courage, the revolutionaries fought gallantly with their pistols and kept the forces at bay till they ran out of ammunition. The battle lasted for about two hours, after which the trench fell silent. Crawling forward slowly, the government troopers peeped into the trench to find one dead and four gravely injured young men. They were not bandits, as the villagers had suspected, but were revolutionaries, led by none other than Bagha Jatin. The dead youth was Chittapriyo. The injured, apart from Jatin himself, were Manoranjan Sengupta, Jyotish and Niren. There were unrecorded casualties on the government side too.

Jatin and the others were shifted to Balasore hospital. Sadly, Bagha Jatin died of gunshot wounds on the next day, 10 September 1915, declining medical help and even water from the British.

Manoranjan and Niren were executed later in Balasore jail while Jyotish was exiled to the Andamans.

Police Commissioner Tegart later confided that, 'If Jatin were an Englishman, then the English people would have built his statue next to Nelson's at Trafalgar Square'. For a change, even Mahatma Gandhi, a fierce proponent of nonviolence, also said that Jatin was a 'Divine personality'.

Bagha Jatin's Escapdes

The reason why such a strong force was in pursuit of five bedraggled youth was because they were chasing Bagha Jatin.

Jatin was born in Kayagram, a village in the Kushtia subdivision of undivided Nadia district (in modern Bangladesh). After completing his school in the village, he went to Calcutta and whilst doing relief work with the Ramakrishna Mission, he came into contact with Sister Nivedita, the Irish disciple of Swami Vivekananda. Through her, he met Swamiji, who left Jatin deeply influenced by his teachings. Swamiji could see zeal and dedication in fiery Jatin and advised him to attend a gym where Jatin learnt and practiced bodybuilding. Jatin suffered a setback when his elder son died at age of six years. Jatin retreated to Hardwar with his wife and children. There he met Swami Bholagiri, who had a calming effect on his troubled mind. Rejuvenated, Jatin came back to plunge into revolution.

Jatin also met Rishi Aurobindo and promised to help an uprising amongst the 'native' soldiers of the British Indian army, as a part of a bigger plan to throw the British out. Jatin was involved in many sedition cases but being a very cautious and a clever young man, he was never indicted. He had many covers too, including the one of a railway contractor. In 1899, Jatin worked as secretary to barrister Pringle Kennedy, founder and editor of the *Trihoot Courrier*. Jatin was greatly influenced by this historian, who, through his editorials and from the Congress platform, argued how urgent it was to have an Indian National Army and to react against the British squandering of their India budget to safeguard their interests in China and elsewhere. Through his contacts with Kennedy, Jatin sent many Indian students to study outside India, establishing a worldwide network.

Siliguri station, 1905.

A young man was rushing to offer water to an ailing lady in the train and he unintentionally brushed against Captain Murphy, a British Army officer. Murphy was accompanied by a few more military personnel. Enraged by the encounter, Murphy uttered some obscenities at the young man. The youth went on to hand over the jug of water to the lady and returned to face the military men and singlehanded, thrashed them in view of a large crowd. The young Indian was Jatin Mukherjee. A case of criminal assault was instituted against him. By the time the case came up for hearing, the incident became a talking point – how an Indian had thrashed the British military men, all by himself. The Magistrate advised Murphy and the others to withdraw the case.

Earlier, in 1905, during the Prince of Wales' visit to Calcutta, Jatin wanted to highlight the plight of Indians. Luck was on his side, when he noticed four British army men sitting on the roof of a fitton and dangling there shodden legs in front of some Indian ladies, seated in the carriage, much to their chagrin. As the convoy of the Prince neared, Jatin jumped up on the carriage roof, slapped the men hard until they fell off the roof. There was a huge commotion, and the reports on the incident were conveyed to the Prince and the Secretary of the State. The Prince didn't mince his words to denounce the attitude of the Englishmen towards the Indian women.

Pursuing his covert revolutionary activities and recruiting likeminded youths into his secret societies, like the Anushilan Samity and Jugantar, Jatin spearheaded many onslaughts against the British. He was arrested repeatedly and released as he ran a loose decentralised organisation and nothing could be proved against him, though he was implicated in most of the covert actions taken against the British, including many heists undertaken to sustain the movements which needed money for purchasing weapons. The cases ran for months, but Jatin had to be released for the lack of 'sufficient evidence'.

By now, Jatin had realised that to attain freedom, a vigorous and extensive armed uprising was necessary. It was imperative to bring all the scattered and small revolutionary outfits in Bengal under one command. The help and cooperation of anti-British countries was also needed. His zeal and leadership qualities attracted many bright young men to his causes.

The first World War broke out in 1914. At that time, Jatin had sent one Jiten Lahiri to Berlin. Upon his return, a fake company called 'Vishnu and Company' was set up to facilitate arms import.

Jatin inspired Rash Behari Bose and M N Roy to contact the Germans. In a meeting, it was decided to form revolutionary committees throughout India, Thailand, Poland, Shanghai, Java and Singapore apart from San Francisco and Berlin. M N Roy's actual name was Naren Bhattacharya. He was out on bail in a dacoity case. Jatin gave him an alias of C Martin and sent him to Batavia, to meet the German Consul there. The Consul took him to one Theodore Helfrik, a German intermediary. Helfrik told Roy that a ship named 'S S Maverick' was already on its way to India with arms and ammunition that Indian revolutionaries had requested for, and was to reach Karachi soon. Roy (Naren) requested Helfrik to divert the ship to Bengal, which the Germans agreed to do. Roy came back and it was decided to anchor the ship near the Sundarbans, where the arms were to be taken off the ship. Extensive plans were laid to destroy the rail lines and the road bridges upon getting hold of the arms as well. Jatin's part was to destroy the Balasore-Madras railway line. But all those plans failed as the Maverick was intercepted on the high seas and seized by the British.

Three more ships, laden with arms, were then planned to be sent to the Odisha coast for the revolutionaries to stage a massive uprising. Jatin and his associates were to meet these ships near Balasore. However, a Czech spy in Europe double-crossed them and alerted the British. The first ship was intercepted near the Andamans, and it never reached the Indian shores. Another came very near the Sundarbans, but due to heavy police presence, turned back. This ended the Indian freedom fighters' German Plan, as it was called.

Another revolutionary called Abani Bannerji was sent to Japan, acting as an agent of Vishnu and company. Nothing much came of that, but Abani met the legendary Chinese leader, Sun Yat Sen. Sun Yat gave him inspiration, fifty pistols, cartridges and money. Rash Behari Bose too, then in east Asia, provided arms to Abani. However, those never reached India, as while coming back, Abani was held in Singapore and after a quick trial, was hanged there.

Meanwhile, Jatin and others were waiting in Kaptipada, in Balasore, when news of the raid on one of the front offices that Jatin had set up in Calcutta came and also the report that the Calcutta police had discovered Jatin's location and were about to arrest him. Jatin, with four of his associates, left his hideout hurriedly and walked for more than two days through Mayurbhanja to Chandabali. They crossed rivers, carrying their arms on their heads, without food. Then they headed for Chasakhand where they were engaged in the trench fight and eventually laid down their lives in the service of their motherland.

There are numerous other stories of Bagha Jatin's revolutionary activities. However, not much has been told about him and his efforts to liberate the motherland; for some inexplicable reasons, historians have deliberately suppressed his rightful place in India's Freedom Story and the credit Bagha Jatin deserves. So, it is incumbent upon us to highlight the life and times of our unsung heroes like Bagha Jatin and many others who contributed to India's struggle for freedom.

THE CHITTAGONG ARMOURY RAID

A simple-looking frail person, with receding hair line and no significant body, was contemplating a revolution on the lines of the IRA.

In the year 1914, on Good Friday, the Irish Republican Army, which was an army of freedom fighters engaged in armed struggle against the British rulers, tried to capture Dublin, Ireland's capital. It was led by Éamon de Valera. Grossly outnumbered, the IRA suffered huge casualties. Many died in the firing, and some were hanged. Though the attempt failed, it sent ripples across the world for the audacity and bravery exhibited by the IRA. Valera, captured and sentenced to

Surya Sen and his group loot the Chittagong armoury

*death, was eventually saved by the USA as he was
a US citizen.*

*After the mutinies of 1857 and 1922, a daring
attempt similar to that of the IRA, was made
in 1930, in Chittagong by a brave group
clamouring for freedom of India. During 1924-
28, the infamous Bengal Ordinance saw many
young Bengali revolutionaries interned in various
jails. While in the jails, the agitating young men
planned to undertake some daring uprisings on
the lines of the IRA, to create fear in the mind of
the British.*

IN 1928, DURING THE Calcutta Congress conclave, Subhas Chandra Bose had raised a uniformed volunteer force and conducted disciplined marches at many places. The idea of such a uniformed army pervaded the minds of young revolutionaries and they dreamt of raising such an indigenous revolutionary army to take up weapons and fight the British forces.

To raise such a force and to muster weapons, huge money was required. It was decided to raise money from relatives and well-wishers. Simultaneously, bombs, pistols, ammunition collection also started.

The place chosen to start the uprising was Chittagong

on India's eastern seaboard. Surya Sen, fondly called Masterda, was chosen as leader of the operation.

Just out of jails, some of the young men like Surya Sen, Ananta Singh, Ganesh Ghosh, Loknath Bal and Ambika Chakravarty had looted 17,000 rupees from the Assam-Bengal Company. The police followed them and after a long-drawn skirmish, they were captured and jailed again. After release, their plan of a nation-wide uprising was speeded up and activities in different fronts, including forming assault groups, commenced. The plan was to raid and take over Raj India's Chittagong Armoury by a swift attack and then install an *independent free Indian government* in Chittagong.

The day chosen was Good Friday, 18 April 1930, precisely at 10 pm. Good Friday was chosen as the IRA had attacked Dublin on that day; as a result the Irish uprising was called the Easter Revolution. On that day in India, most British officers were expected to be busy in the festivities.

Chittagong (now in Bangladesh) is an ancient port city of historical importance. It has a recorded history since the fourth century BC. It was under successive Bengal dynasties till the Sultan of Bengal annexed it in 1340. Arab Muslims and Persians frequented the town for trade, and many settled here, making the area Muslim dominated.

Thus, Chittagong soon became a gateway of trading for China, Sumatra, Sri Lanka, Maldives and Africa and the port and the town flourished.

Over the years, it was visited by many famous persons of the times like Ibn Batuta, Xuanzang, Nicolo de'Conti (from Venice) and many others. In 1528, the Portuguese established the first European colony in Bengal, and it controlled Chittagong for more than a hundred years. They imposed taxes on ships of other countries and fought dissenters. The Mughals, after a fierce battle, wrested Chittagong from the Portuguese.

In 1685, the English East India Company tried unsuccessfully to gain control over this port. Their attempts continued till 1793, when finally, the Company Bahadur managed to seize the port on the Bay of Bengal. The British established a huge armoury in the city as the port afforded easy shipment and the East India Company faced war and rebellion. During the 1857 mutiny, three regiments of the Bengal infantry here revolted and released all the prisoners from jail. They were later suppressed by other regiments loyal to the empire.

Chittagong was very crucial to the British and their ships lay in the port with supplies throughout the year. During the freedom movement, Chittagong became one of the major centres supplying revolutionaries and soon it was to be witness to a stunning act of daredevilry by youths of the town and its vicinity. A large number of young men from undivided East Bengal, Dhaka, Chittagong and other areas opted for armed revolution to free India from colonial rule and gave their lives to the cause of free India.

Surya Sen was born in 1894 in Chittagong district. He was a schoolteacher, which earned him the affectionate sobriquet of 'Masterda'. He was a brilliant organiser and an exemplary leader. He had turned to revolutionary ideals while he himself was a student and had joined the revolutionary organisation, Anushilan Samiti. His brilliant strategy-making skills, daring, humanism, seniority, and a very unassuming nature made him the automatic leader of the group which was to embark upon the armoury raid at Chittagong. Surya Sen soon became the Secretary of the Chittagong District Congress Committee. Throughout Bengal, the Congress party was made a base and cover for recruiting bright and brave young boys. The local physical activity clubs also scouted for volunteers.

The plan of the armoury raid included raiding the police armoury in the town, seizing control of the armoury, taking over the auxiliary armoury and looting arms and ammunition from both armouries, cutting off all communication systems to the town like telephones, telegraph lines and railways. This would have meant isolation of Chittagong from the rest of British India. It was decided to unfurl an 'Indian' flag and declare Chittagong an independent town.

The plan was elaborate and utter secrecy was required. The British used to plant decoys to extract information about all such plans that the revolutionaries made. It was therefore necessary to filter the volunteers carefully and choose the best amongst them. It was also imperative to keep spreading misinformation, to fool the infiltrators planted by police. The covert action was to be of paramount importance to the revolutionaries. Its success meant a big glory while failure was to be paid by losing young lives and breaking the morale of the movement.

All revolutionary army members were to wear khaki uniforms. Squads were made out of a 65-member team that included young women, all chosen on the basis of loyalty, daring, physical fitness, access and exposure to arms and most of all, the willingness to die in order to liberate the motherland.

Thirty-two young men were placed in the first squad responsible for raiding the Police Lines and the armoury, under the leadership of Ananta Singh and Ganesh Ghosh, two senior leaders.

The second squad of six men was to attack and seize the auxiliary armoury, under Loknath Bal.

The third squad of six men was to seize the telephone and telegraph offices.

A fourth squad, also of six men, was responsible for attacking the European Club in the town.

The remaining cadre were divided in two squads, with the aim of cutting off Chittagong from the rest of the country by disrupting rail and telegraph lines.

Most of the militants were between 14 to 18 years old.

At the appointed date and time, the teams gathered at the Congress office in Chittagong, in twos and threes, and set off for the armoury area on foot. They wore shirts and dhutis over their uniforms. They had side bags for carrying bullets after the loot and some essentials. The raiders were to wait near the armoury for the signal to attack at the predestined time of ten pm.

Then came information that the assault had to be delayed by one hour. It was difficult for the members assembled there to wait there for so long as the neighbourhood was suspicious of these young men. It had so happened that the group leaders were to come in taxis, hijacked after sedating the drivers with chloroform. Being a festival day and the number of taxis being limited in the town, it became difficult to get hold of taxis. Finally, several taxis were located, and the Sikh drivers were overpowered, sedated with chloroform, gagged and bound and interned in an isolated house. Valuable time was lost thus.

The leaders, dressed in full khaki uniforms and wearing insignias, drove up smartly to the armoury's main gate. Ananta Singh and Ganesh Ghosh sat on the front seat. The gate was manned by armed sentries. Seeing the car with officers they thought were from the army, the sentries saluted and proceeded to open the gates.

One of the sentries came forward to enquire. At this point, he was fired upon, and he fell to the ground shouting, *'Gandhi baba ka raaj ho gaya'*. This was answered by the revolutionaries with a loud slogan of Vande Mataram, which was a signal for the others to join.

The shouts of Vande Mataram and 'down with imperialism' resonated all over, making people think that the entire valley was surrounded by a huge revolutionary force, heavily armed. The young revolutionaries ran into the armoury, firing here and there with their personal guns and pistols, shouting Vande Mataram. The action had begun. The hillock behind the armoury housed the Police Lines, with around six hundred Gurkha and Bihari policemen in the barracks. The gun fire, shouts and panic-filled voices of their colleagues from the armoury made them fearful. Thinking that Swadeshi revolutionaries had encircled and captured the lines, the men in the barracks ran helter-skelter. They fled to the jungles and bushes behind the armoury, leaving the armoury unguarded.

By now, the raiders had broken the heavy locks of the armoury with sledgehammers. The armoury had guns which were good for one shot at a time, like old muskets. They were too heavy to be carried along on shoulders. Still, the guns were taken out and search for their ammunition was made. They were not to be found. Time was ticking away. Suddenly, Ganesh Ghosh shouted, 'Company fall in'. The entire group came to a line formation, like in formal armies. Ghosh picked up a rifle and showed everyone how to use it, very like a musket. Everyone loaded their guns and aimed at the skies. 'Fire', came the command. With that, the rifles boomed in unison, filling the skies over Chittagong with gunfire. They did this three times.

By then, Loknath Bal and the youth leader Nirmal Sen had reached the auxiliary force armoury. There too, a rifle-toting sentry came forward to salute, taking them to be army officers. The revolutionaries fired but were stopped by the other sentries. The in-charge, Sergeant Major Farell, who was having dinner with his wife, ran in brandishing a pistol only to be shot at fatally. Before dying, he asked his wife to ring up the police. The phone lines were disconnected by that time. Six sentries lay dead and several lay injured.

The auxiliary armoury had Lewis guns and ten-shot muskets. They were invaluable at that moment. The doors were broken, the guns taken but there were no cartridges for them. Without cartridges, the guns were useless.

By that time, three other curious British officers had come out, they too faced rebel firing. One fell injured and the others ran away in the darkness of the night. Frustrated by not getting the ammunition, Loknath Bal ordered the armoury to be set on fire. Then the group headed to the main armoury where the other groups joined them.

The third group, consisting of the most daring six members, reached the European Club to mount an attack. As the plan was delayed by over an hour, the club was deserted; it was Good Friday and people had gone home. The attack on the European Club was planned to kill as many British officers as possible – to avenge the killings of innocent people at Chauri Chaura and at other places. Being Good Friday, it was expected that many officers would be there. Due to the delay in the attack, this plan went awry.

The telephone and telegraph lines were cut off, and the railway lines were uprooted as planned.

Regardless of several setbacks, the raiders assembled at the central square in the Police Lines. The free 'Indian' flag was hoisted with gun salutes. A provisional government was formed with Surya Sen as the Commander-in-Chief. A guard of honour was presented to him with shouts of, 'Inquilab Zindabad, Chattagram Republican Army Zindabad'.

Suddenly, a machine gun fire rattled the group. The firing came from an elevated water tank. Taking prone positions, the revolutionaries fired their rifles at the tank, silencing the guns there. The leaders now apprehended that there might be other gunmen from the British side, lying in wait to retaliate. A decision was taken not to confront them with mere one-shot rifles and revolvers. The looted guns without ammunition and the Police Lines were ordered to be burned.

The responsibility to do so was with one Himanshu Sen.

While pouring petrol all over, Himanshu did not notice that petrol had fallen on his own clothes. The clothes caught fire and before others could react, he got burnt badly.

He was whisked away to the town in a car by Ananta Singh, Ganesh Ghosh and two others. The main group waited for them to be back for some time, and then fearing police attack, decided to move on without them. The hills once again resonated with the cries of, 'Chattagram Youth Revolution Zindabad. Long Live Revolution' as the group left for the nearby hills.

Surya Sen decided not to fight openly with the huge force in the town as the group would have been grossly outnumbered. The swiftness and suddenness of their attack initially numbed the government forces. However, it was sure that the forces would regroup and engage the revolutionaries.

The policemen who had abandoned the Lines had also taken shelter in the hillocks and bushes in the neighbourhood, stunned by the swiftness of the attack and remained under the impression that the Police Lines and armoury were under Swadeshi control. They hid in the bushes without food or water for two nights, until more government troops arrived in the town on the third day.

So, for three days, Chittagong remained cut off from the world and the only contact was made from a ship anchored at the port. The administration thought that the revolutionaries were manning the huge armoury and were scattered throughout the town and avoided any action, without concrete information. Therefore, Chittagong was a free town for about three days with the Indian flag flying audaciously, hoisted by a motley group of 'do or die' revolutionaries, led by a resolute commander, Masterda.

The revolutionaries had, however, left town and the groups moved on during the night, crossing the small hillocks and by the dawn of 20 April, they had stopped on a hillock with thick vegetation. This was a good hiding place. At noon, while the group was resting under the shades of trees, two men appeared from behind the bushes. Caught unawares, they were nervous and said that they were cowherds looking for their cows. The men aroused suspicions, as there were no signs of any cow since the morning and the men were too old to be cowherds. They were brought to Surya Sen. Looking at the group and the arms, the men confessed that they were police spies on the lookout for the revolutionaries.

Some group members wanted to kill the two men so that the location of their hideout was not revealed. However, Surya Sen and Nirmal Sen advised against it, as firing would have alerted nearby villages. The men were left unharmed, with a warning not to expose the group (surprisingly, at the trials later, the two informers refused to identify the members arrested).

The groups proceeded towards another hillock in the morning, with parched throats and tired legs. They stopped briefly while Surya Sen and Ambika Chakravarty showed the boys how to use the guns looted from the armoury. Though they were single-shot muskets, their range was long. Trained, the groups trudged ahead and came across a watermelon field. Thirsty and hungry, they plucked a few ripe melons and ate them. The field watchman, a young man, came running to stop them but seeing the group with guns, stopped abruptly. He could sense that the group had just done some daring deed and offered the group more melons. Thanking the man, Sen and his companions crossed the hills and by dawn took shelter in a hillock full of trees and bushes.

The British administration had by now spread out their informers and spies across the countryside, and by noon, a plane circled overhead to locate the revolutionaries. This was an uncommon sight and the villagers from nearby areas thronged to see the low-flying plane. This posed a danger to the group, and they did not move till night. Hungry and thirsty, they sent a couple of boys to get whatever they could from the village shops, even at the risk of being spotted. Ambika, who knew the area, volunteered and after a long search returned with some *khichri* (a cooked dish of rice and lentils), to the great relief of the group.

Surya Sen and his teams, of course, realised that the police were in hot pursuit. Moreover, four of the leaders – Ananta Singh, Ganesh Ghosh, Ananda Gupta and Jibon Ghosal – all senior leaders, had got separated from the main group as they had taken the burnt youth into town, to a hospital. Ananta and others had not yet re-joined Surya Sen's main group. Sen decided to send a young man called Amarendra Nandi – a brave and clever local youth – to go into the town and gather information about police activities and the other four leaders. Amarendra never returned. Amarendra, after entering the town, was unable to leave the town due to heavy police presence. When he tried to sneak out, he was surrounded by police and military personnel, led by senior police officials. He took position under a culvert with two revolvers in his hands. Urged to surrender and to throw away the arms, his reply came through bullets. Eventually, he was captured by the police and severely tortured for information. Instead of divulging the whereabouts of the revolutionaries, he consumed potassium cyanide and died in custody. Oblivious of this, the revolutionaries wearily marched on during the night of 20 April and again stopped for the day on a hillock.

Tired and starving, they again came across a watermelon field. The owner, an elderly Muslim, knowing fully about the group and their daring acts, offered them few watermelons free of cost. The group rested under the shade. Surya Sen and Nirmal Sen, the two senior leaders, cut the melons into small pieces and distributed them amongst the sixty members. The melons were not enough for them. The leaders took the skin and chewed them, giving the juicy part to the juniors. This act of sacrifice emboldened the young members.

Night descended and the group marched forward. They lost their way as there was no track. Backtracking, they took another path. Dawn was near and shelter had to be found at the earliest: They saw a small hillock with some tree cover, though it was not enough to hide sixty men. The hillock was surrounded by rice fields and there was a pond at the foothill. The hillock had higher hills around it. This was the Jalalabad hills where history was to be written on that day.

The Battle of Jalalabad

As daylight broke on 22 April, ordinary farmers were on their way to their rice and melon fields unaware that around them, the not-too-distant hills would soon resound with fierce gun battles between freedom fighters and India's colonial rulers. The large group of revolutionaries had under cover of darkness hastened to reach the hillock and use it for whatever shelter it offered. Reaching there, the group scattered in twos and fours. They rested, cleaned their weapons, and got ready for all possible action.

The senior leaders discussed the strategy ahead. It was clear that to mount a frontal attack on Chittagong, as originally planned, was suicidal due to lack of ammunition. There was no point in waiting for Ananta Singh and the other leaders, as three days had passed by now. It was certain that by then, the police and army would have mustered their resources and would soon mount a massive attack.

At noon, a man was sighted on a hill beyond, looking

at the hillock and signalling to someone with a piece of cloth. The group were alerted. Meanwhile, a train passed by, behind the hills and stopped. There was no station for the train to have stopped. Surya Sen knew that the line must have been repaired and government forces had arrived. He ordered the members to get ready and take position all around for an imminent battle.

Masterda was correct. By 5 pm, a huge police force was visible all around, armed to the teeth. 'Get ready for the ultimate fight with the British imperial army and let us see who wins this day. We are revolutionaries. Let the world witness this historical day.' Saying this, Surya Sen appointed Loknath Bal, a fearless and strong young man, as the Commander in the coming battle. Loknath gratefully accepted this assignment and promised to fight till the last, along with his committed soldiers, the men he had groomed over the years.

'Get ready and take lying positions in your sections. Remember, we revolutionaries have never lowered our heads to the British. Today is no exception', saying this, Loknath took up his own firing position, followed by his mentors Surya Sen and Nirmal Sen.

The army and police forces moved in as the revolutionaries took up their stand, shoulder to shoulder, in prone positions. They had the advantage of being at a higher level. Shortly, heavy firing from both sides commenced. The rifles that the revolutionaries had were effective but, after a shot was fired from them, it took time for re-firing. The hills resonated with the cries of Vande Mataram and Bharat Mata ki Jai, alongside the wheezing bullets and sound of machine gun fire. The British forces, at a lower height and in the open, were at serious disadvantage. It was an advantage to the novice revolutionaries, and heavy casualties were reported in the British troops. The first round of the unequal battle was won by the untrained boys. The trained force had to retreat.

There was an eerie pause as the guns fell silent and the fighting sides rearranged themselves.

By now, many British force personnel had climbed on to the higher hills, which afforded them a clear view of the revolutionary group. Machine guns were placed in higher positions and heavy firing commenced. This sudden attack caught the revolutionaries unaware and soon, quite a few of them died. The remaining young men scrambled to find cover. Intense firing continued. Surya Sen directed the group not to let the forces at lower levels come near; at the same time save themselves from the gun fire from the higher hills.

As anticipated by Masterda, the British forces kept approaching through the rice fields, confident of their machine gun cover. The moment they were within firing range, Loknath shouted, 'Halt'. The British troops stopped momentarily, confounded even as Loknath gave the long-awaited command, 'Fire, Volley fire'. The rifles fired in unison. The British troopers ran back, some men rolling down the hillock, gravely injured or dead.

The Jalalabad hills again resonated with victory cries from the revolutionaries. The British, surprised by the onslaught, regrouped and circling around retook positions on the higher hills, this time giving them a vantage position. They mounted more machine guns there and launched a vicious volley of fire.

Loknath ordered the boys to lie down and save themselves till darkness descended. However, the advancing British forces did not allow any respite.

Meanwhile, another problem cropped up. The barrels of the rifles were getting unbearably hot and holding the guns was becoming tough. Surya Sen and Nirmal Sen started rolling over to the riflemen to clean and cool the barrels with lubricating oil.

Loknath Bal's younger brother, Tegra, was full of vigour and zeal. He defied the orders to lie low. In a bid to fire directly at the machine gun positions of the British, he stood up to locate their position. Within no time, a hail of bullets riddled his body. He called out to his brother and told him to continue the fight. Tegra Bal was just fourteen years old.

One by one, the daring ones fell to the incessant machine gun fire from a higher level. Tripura Sen, Bidhu Bhattacharya, Ardhendu Dastidar. Ardhendhu was wrapped in bandages as he was injured badly while making bombs. He insisted on joining battle despite being in severe pain. Such was his love for the motherland.

At one stage, one of the revolutionaries, Binod Dutta, though severely injured, faced problems with his rifle. He looked around for a rifle. Surya Sen handed him one from Pravas Bal, who lay dead nearby. Binod found this rifle too jammed. There was no lubricant nearby. Precious time ticked away. Binod took Pravas' blood and used it as lubrication. The rifle boomed again.

As dusk descended, the intensity of the battle abated. The British had thought that the revolutionaries had other groups lurking nearby and they would mount an attack. This miscalculation made the British forces withdraw for the night, leaving their dead in the rice fields.

Surya Sen decided to leave the hillock under the cover of night. The group counted their dead. There were twelve dead bodies lying on that hillock including a 14 years old boy's. The bodies were lined up and were given gun salute by the remaining members. One of the seniormost members,

Ambika Chakravarty lay against a huge tree, profusely bleeding from his head and looked listless. Presumed dead, he was left there to be in peace.

It was 1930 and not the northern hills of the 1830s, where the British had once fought the Marathas, the Persians, the Afghans and the Sikhs. The hills of the eastern Jalalabad too witnessed history being written by a group of young men, driven by the love for motherland and the will to free her.

Next morning, the British mounted an attack again, firing heavily and encircling the hillock. There was no response from the revolutionaries. The forces reached the top to only find a dozen dead bodies strewn all over. The bodies were put in a trench, pieces of wood were placed over the pile and a fire was lit to burn these bodies. Two young men were found seriously injured but alive. They were moved to hospitals.

Acknowledging their bravery, the British forces gave the bodies a last salute and took off their hats. It was a rare gesture accorded by the British lions to Bengal's tiger cubs who had fought to their last breath, making the supreme sacrifice for a free India at the dawn of their lives.

Post-Jalalabad and the Aftermath

The group which had left the Jalalabad hills trudged through thorny bushes, moving at a fast pace. They had only pond water to drink.

Next morning, it rained heavily. The group had to lie on their bullets and guns, to keep them dry and ready for action. They got drenched and it slowed them down. A plane hovered above to locate the group but could not spot them. The revolutionaries then split into smaller groups, allowing each group to chalk out its own fate. Surya Sen, with Nirmal Sen and Loknath Bal, took shelter in one of the villages where a group member, Subodh Roy, had a house. They left this shelter after a couple of days when the hunt had slowed.

Though the main group and most of the young men with Surya Sen managed to get to some safe haven, the four, who had taken the burnt body of Himanshu Sen into the city, were nowhere to be seen. Four days had passed.

Putiyari Railway Station, near Chittagong.

Four villagers stood huddled near the ticket counter. One of them stepped out to get their tickets. After the four villagers had boarded the train, a suspicious Station Master who had heard of the Chittagong uprising, conveyed his concern to the Guard of the outgoing train. He also sent telegrams to the approaching stations.

The train stopped at Feni station where a big posse of policemen boarded the compartment and asked the villagers to get down. The men were marched to the Station Master's room where they were interrogated. After failing to elicit information, the police resorted to body search. At this point, the villagers pulled out their revolvers and fired. One of the villagers had gone out with two policemen to attend to a call of nature. He too pulled out a revolver and began firing at the policemen. Taking advantage of darkness, the four villagers ran away. They were the four senior leaders, now disguised as villagers, who had got separated from the main group in Chittagong.

After the Jalalabad battle, the leadership debated their further course of action. The young ones were impatient and itching to engage in more audacious attacks; they wanted to take revenge for the death of their friends in the Jalalabad battle. They requested Masterda to allow them to attack the European Club once again as the plan on the day of the armoury attack had not succeeded.

Initially reluctant, Masterda allowed another attempt at killing British officers at the club. Thus, on 5 May 1930, six fully armed young men made a second attempt to breach the club. They failed as the club was now highly fortified by the military.

Having failed to enter the club, this group took shelter in the house of an acquaintance and had just sat down to a meal when someone noticed policemen converging on the house. Within minutes, the young men ran out of the house through the rear door with police in hot pursuit. The group got into a boat on the Karnafuli river and were halfway across by the time a police launch caught up with them. The police maintained a distance, fearing firing from the fearless youths. Undaunted, the youths rowed in a zig zag manner and vanished in the reeds on the other bank.

Exasperated, the police did what they did best. They spread a rumour in the villages across the river that there were some dacoits on the loose. Information about them was to be rewarded amply. The simple villagers believed that and chased the youths. The revolutionaries had to fire at the villagers to scare them. In the darkness of night, the young men lost their way and the police caught up with them. In the resulting firing, two revolutionaries got injured and were apprehended. The other four escaped and reached a village by daybreak. They were hungry and tired. Knocking at a door, they faced an old woman who, having guessed their identity, offered them food. The youth waited in the bushes as the woman cooked. Unfortunately, before they could be served, they were spotted by a villager. Hearing his shouts, the police encircled the youths and placed machine guns and riflemen all around.

In the reeds and bushes Rajat, Swadesh, Manoranjan and Deboprasad took out their revolvers and took up positions. The officers ordered the boys to surrender, which the boys refused to do. On being told that death was the only thing which awaited them, Manoranjan replied, 'Manoranjan does not know how to surrender. I want to be Jatin Mukherji of Balasore'. This enraged the police and they began shooting. Just four revolvers and a few bullets against dozens of rifles and machine guns; time was running out for the boys.

'Come on, we are not surrendering to the hated imperial power. I shall fire at Deboprasad, and then Rajat will fire at me. Like this, we will kill each other rather than surrender,' Manoranjan said. So, they fired at each other. Swadesh, Rajat and Manoranjan died instantly while a grievously injured Deboprasad awaited death.

Asked whether Deboprasad wanted to say some last words to the police chief present there, he roared, 'Which chief? That Lowman? I would have shot him, had I not injured my hand'. This brave son of India breathed his last after saying this. Deboprasad's last wish of eliminating Lowman was fulfilled within three months.

In the meantime, Loknath Bal moved into a safe house in French Chandannagor. Being a very attractive personality like Subhas Bose, he used to get spotted quickly. So, he lay low in the French colony for a while. However, the ever-sniffing Charles Tegart, the hound of Bengal police, surrounded the house one night on the first of September

1930. There were four revolvers against dozens of guns when the encounter between the revolutionaries and the police occurred. Ultimately Lokenath Bal, Ganesh Ghosh and Ananda Gupta were arrested, along with the owners of the house. However, Jivan Ghosal was killed in the encounter.

A few days later, Ambika Chakravarty, the one who was left behind on the Jalalabad hills, presumed dead, was also apprehended. Ambika, who had a head injury, had regained consciousness during the night and had painfully staggered to a village nearby and was given refuge in the barn of a friendly Muslim landlord. Upon recovery, he had moved to the town and was caught.

Ananta Singh inexplicably surrendered. With this, most of the leading members of the Chittagong armoury raid were either dead or behind bars.

Surya Sen and Nirmal Sen remained elusive.

Surya Sen had eluded police hunts a number of times. In 1924, his hideout was encircled by the police. It was dusk and Surya Sen, having the benefit of a lean person, slithered down the toilet hole which used to be quite wide in those days. Climbing down, he disappeared under the descending darkness into the jungle.

Then, in 1926, his safehouse was again surrounded by police. There was no escape route. He threw away his dress and shoes and, wearing a very dirty vest, he threw a dirty towel over his shoulders. Thus disguised, with a tea kettle in hand, he climbed down the stairs, a distraught look on his face. He was accosted by a policeman who stopped him. Surya Sen told the policeman that he was a tea supplier who had come to collect his money. The policeman was adamant. He did not allow Surya Sen to leave. Sen feigned fear and started shivering. An officer looked at him with disdain, measured him up and finding a lean, thin villager-type of man, asked him to leave the premises as a gun fight had started. Surya Sen ran out and within minutes he was in a safe territory. The policemen did not realise that their prize catch was again out of their reach. His frail, simple looks helped him in such daring escapes.

Surya Sen and several other senior leaders evaded arrest for three long years. By then the reward for giving information on Surya Sen had climbed to ten thousand rupees, a huge sum in those days. During a close encounter in 1932, the police had nearly caught Surya Sen. However, at that time he had escaped by jumping from the first floor of a safehouse, along with his close disciple Preetilata Waddedar. Surya Sen was given cover fire by Nirmal Sen, who engaged in a gunfight with the police and got killed in the process.

Betrayed

In February 1933, very ill, Masterda took refuge in Gairala village, in the house of his distant cousin, Brajen Sen.

Brajen's cousin, Netra Sen, wanted the reward amount. Netra had got suspicious when he noticed that some outsiders were staying in one of the houses in the village. Curious, he asked the lady who took food to the visitors, about their identity. She proudly disclosed that she was cooking for Masterda and his associates. Netra, greedy for the reward, informed the police which lost no time in getting into action.

On the night of the sixteenth of February, the police and the army surrounded Brajen's house with machine guns and rifles. The place was illuminated with search lights and illumination rockets. Heavy firing started from both sides. The house had Surya Sen, Kalpana Dutta and two other revolutionaries, all carrying revolvers. Despite the heavy gunfire from the police force, Masterda and the others managed to sneak out of the house. All of them escaped. Only Masterda, too ill to move properly, was caught by a Gurkha soldier and arrested just a few meters from the house.

All the senior police officers made a beeline to Chittagong to have a look at Surya Sen when he was brought in. They were surprised to see a diminutive figure with receding hairline and bright eyes who, now in chains, had made the forces look like fools for three years. The commander and mastermind of several anti-British actions including the Chittagong raid stood before all, like a caged tiger. Typical to their style, despite the sermons they gave the world on human rights, the British administration and its police engaged in immeasurable cruelty, kicking, whipping and abusing the ill man with animal brutality before taking him to jail.

Betrayer Netra collected his reward and was very happy. His happiness, however, did not last long.

About a week after Surya Sen was arrested, a young man barged into Netra's house. Netra's wife was serving him food at the time. The intruder jumped at Netra and in a flash, beheaded him with a sickle. The traitor lay dead in a pool of blood. The police came and asked his wife if she had seen the killer. The wife denied having seen the killer. She stood firm on her version, though the police pressurised her for the details. The killer was none other than Netra's own nephew. He had taken revenge on behalf of the entire village, to atone for the treachery against Masterda by one of them.

In the organisation, Tarkeshwar Dastidar took over Masterda's place as leader. Efforts to get Masterda out of jail by attacking it were made but it failed. Tarkeshwar Dastidar and Kalpana Dutta were arrested after a gunfight with the police, which left two other revolutionaries dead.

Surya Sen, Tarkeshwar Dastidar and Kalpana Dutta were tried by a Special Tribunal in a secluded house. The cases against Surya Sen were many and the British felt humiliated about the Chittagong episode. The ruling came as expected. Surya Sen and Tarkeshwar Dastidar were sentenced to death by hanging and Kalpana Dutta was sentenced for life.

On 12 January 1933, when the clock struck twelve at night, a few British police officers and sergeants entered the cells of Surya Sen and Tarkeshwar. With animal brutality they showered blows on the hapless men breaking their bones, heads and fingers. Then their teeth were broken and pulled out with hammer and tongs. Such brutality was unprecedented, and the jail premises reverberated with their cries of agony. The half-dead bodies of the two martyrs were then dragged out to be hanged.

The bodies of Surya Sen, Commander and President of Free Chittagong, symbolising India's quest for freedom, along with his worthy companion Tarkeshwar, were put in sacks, taken out on a ship and dumped into the ocean two hundred nautical miles away from the shores while the city of Chittagong slept.

This ended an important chapter of Indian freedom struggle.

THE VERANDAH BATTLE

There were quite a number of failed and aborted missions after the Chittagong armoury raid, which were huge setbacks for the young revolutionaries. They were itching for a successful mission which could bring fear into the minds of the British. 29 August 1930. Dhaka in erstwhile undivided Bengal. The Inspector General of Police, F J Lowman, along with local Superintendent of Police, E Hudson, was visiting an officer who was ill in Dhaka's Mitford hospital which is a part of the Sir Salimullah Medical College. Lowman was a hardliner and a strict policeman. When Lowman and Hudson were coming out of

Three daredevils fight with a strong police force

the cabin after the visit, they were accosted by a fourth-year medical college student at the hospital, Binoy Bose.

Binoy brandished a revolver and before anyone could react, shot Lowman and Hudson at point blank range. Both collapsed and lay in a pool of blood while Binoy made a spectacular escape, mingling with the curious crowd. Deboprasad's last wish was, thus, fulfilled.

AFTER FIRING AT LOWMAN and Hudson, Binoy ran through the hospital gardens. He climbed on the boundary wall, jumped over to an adjacent building and vanished. Lowman died two days later while Hudson survived. A massive but futile manhunt was undertaken. The administration resorted to inhuman torture of the local people and hospital witnesses in order to apprehend Binoy. They could only find out that he was a student of the fourth year of medical studies. The hunt for Binoy continued. A reward money of rupees ten thousand was announced for any information leading to Binoy and his capture.

Dolaigunj station.

It was the first station after Dhaka. Two poor-looking Muslim villagers were waiting on the platform for the train to Narayanganj. They wore torn vests, dirty lungis and held tattered bags. The train arrived, but the waiting passengers were not allowed in till the bogies were searched thoroughly for Binoy. The passengers were allowed to board the train only after a thorough search. The two villagers sat huddled in a corner of one compartment, staring with blank faces. The compartment was full of young boys from the Dhaka University, making merry. In fact, they had been asked to provide cover for the two villagers by their student organisation.

Before the train reached Narayanganj, a whistle blew. It was a signal of imminent danger. The entire compartment was quickly vacated as the train slowed at the outer signal. A police party waited at the station for rechecking.

The underground members of the Narayanganj revolutionary group took the villagers to a safe house. Next day, dressed as local businessmen, the two crossed the Meghna River by steamer. Reaching Kishoregunj station, they found it buzzing with policemen. Unmoved, the two, once again dressed as poor villagers, approached a ticket checker and acted as innocent villagers looking to buy tickets for Calcutta. The checker took pity and took them to the counter, walking them through the police posse. They boarded the train only to find a police inspector with his two sepoys enter the compartment at the next station. One of the villagers lay down instantly, with a sheet over himself while the other stood by, looking distressed. The inspector sat on a bench. He got suspicious and asked why the man was covering himself like that. The villager, standing with folded hands, told the inspector that it was his nephew suffering from smallpox, a dreaded infectious disease in those days. Fearing infection, the inspector changed his compartment at the next station. The villagers were Binoy and his companion Supati Roy, a senior revolutionary.

Thus, they reached Calcutta safely and hid in a safe house. The top leaders of Bengal Volunteers – the revolutionary organisation Binoy was connected to – were not in favour of Binoy being kept in Calcutta. Charles Tegart, the Police chief, was spreading his spy network to nab Binoy. A 10,000-rupee award had been announced for his capture or information on Binoy. All the outbound trains from Calcutta were being checked intensively to stop Binoy Bose from slipping out.

Bandel, a junction station near Calcutta.

There were searchlights everywhere. A car approached the barrier. It was the car of the District Magistrate. His personal assistant, Saroj Roy, sat in the vehicle, with two people. The policemen stood to alert and saluted. Saroj Roy instructed the police to be vigilant and not allow the man with a ten thousand rupees reward on him to escape. Saroj Roy's guests boarded the out bound train and waved to Roy.

The police could not guess that the guests were none other than a top leader of the Bengal Volunteers, a mastermind of the Rodda arms heist (Haridas Datta) and accompanying him was Binoy Bose. Saroj Roy, a government official, had taken grave risks in helping the two revolutionaries escape.

Binoy stayed in a colliery safe house near Dhanbad – not for long, though. He was impatient to act. He again moved to Calcutta. Subhas Chandra Bose was of the opinion that Binoy should go to Europe or America as chances of him being caught were high. Haridas Datta approached a senior dock official, one Mr Mills, and arranged for Binoy's voyage to Italy by a cargo ship.

The plan was ready, but Binoy stubbornly refused. He offered himself for a bigger piece of action. That was an attack on the Writers Building, the heart of the empire. Binoy was still itching to act against imperialist Britain.

Dalhousie Square again. The administrative headquarters of the British empire in Bengal was housed in a majestic building called the Writers Building, not far from where the Rodda & Co arms heist had taken place a few years earlier. It was the headquarters of the police force of undivided Bengal too and remains present-day Kolkata's prestigious office area.

8 December 1930.

On that mildly cold day, the nerve center of the colonial

Bengal government was, as usual, buzzing with European officers, Indian officials, commoners. The Inspector General of Prisons, Col N S Simpson, was busy in his huge office. Simpson was a rough and tough policeman who excelled in torturing jail inmates, especially those who had rebelled against Britain.

Three young men, attired in European clothing, slowly walked down the long verandah (corridor), talking in low voices. They stopped in front of Simpson's office, looked around and then like flying arrows, entered Simpson's office. 'Pray to your God Colonel. Your time is over' thundered one, while three revolvers pumped bullets into Simpson. Simpson slumped in his chair, stone dead. The youth ran out, mingling with people panicking after the firing in the busiest government building in the city.

After killing Simpson in the Writers Building, Binoy and his two associates entered the passport office next door and fired at some officers there. Then they ran out into the verandah facing the street. By then, there was a huge commotion. Hearing the firing, and the alarmed cries of people, a large police posse had also gathered on the street. As they came out into the corridor, the three young revolutionaries faced firing from the police posse across them. Within no time, the dreaded officer Charles Tegart also reached the spot and joined the force, with his men.

The valiant three fired back from prone positions they had taken up. The unequal battle lasted for quite some time and stopped only when the revolutionaries had exhausted their ammunition.

The battle was nearing end, even as a huge crowd watched. While Binoy and Dinesh were left with one bullet each, Badal had none. The trio ran back into the building, to a vacant room and bolted it from inside. They decided to kill themselves rather than get caught and face police brutalities. All of them had potassium cyanide ampoules with them. Shouting Vande Mataram, which resounded through the building, they decided to consume poison. Binoy and Dinesh placed their revolvers on their heads and pressed the triggers. The room fell silent. The police, too stunned by the turn of events, did not dare to enter the room for quite some time. A group of gun-toting policemen broke open the massive door to find the bodies on the floor. Badal was dead. Dinesh had a bullet through his neck. Binoy had a bullet in his temple. Dinesh and Binoy had not been able to chew their cyanide ampoules. Both were alive and breathing faintly. They were shifted to the hospital, but not before some British officers, including the infamous Tegart, trampled on the bodies and limbs of the grievously injured men out of frustration. The three brave hearts were Binoy Bose, Dinesh Gupta and Badal

Gupta. Binoy had killed Lowman and Simpson and also eluded arrest for long, so he was tortured more.

'Battle of Verandah', *The Statesman* newspaper carried this headline the day after the gunfight in Writers Building. It also wrote,

'Lt Col N S Simpson was shot dead. Mr J W Nelson, Judicial Secretary, was wounded in the leg. Another bullet narrowly missed Mr A Marr, the Finance member, who on hearing the shots, came to the door of his room. An orderly of the DPI was wounded in the leg. Passerby were dumbfounded to see in broad daylight in the heart of the business quarters of Calcutta an incident that had all the elements of a Chicago gunning affair'.

The Writers building was till recently the Secretariat of West Bengal.

In honour of the three brave revolutionaries, Dalhousie Square was named BBD Bagh.

However, the feats of Binoy, Badal and Dinesh remain unknown to people beyond Bengal and it is time that they get a place in the national narrative.

Binoy Krishna Basu was 22 years old when he died. A medical student in Dhaka, he joined a secret society connected to the revolutionary Jugantar party, which inspired and trained numerous such motivated youths to die for the freedom of the motherland through armed struggle. In hospital, under heavy security, his condition deteriorated as he intentionally enlarged his wounds by inserting his fingers into them. The wounds became septic, and Binoy went into a coma. A priest sent to him for last prayers was surprised to hear Binoy murmuring, 'Halt, fire, glory to motherland'. His parents were allowed to meet him, and he responded by moving his head upon being called by his parents. His father was an accomplished hunter and hardly missed his targets. His son also did not miss his targets. The anguished but proud parents watched their loving son dying for his motherland.

Binoy died in his sleep, depriving his captors the pleasure of executing him.

On 14 December, the bravest of the braves, was cremated in the presence of admiring policemen and a sea of people – all in tears.

Dinesh Gupta was 19 years old when he was hanged. He was a member of the Bengal Volunteers. Dinesh was a well-built, fearless youth; he was a poet, philosopher, writer and artist. His stories had been published in leading magazines of that time. Dinesh Gupta translated a short story by Anton Chekhov which was published in *Probasi* magazine. Moreover, he excelled in organising and motivating youth for the causes of the motherland with his emotional public addresses and logic. He established the Midnapore branch of the Bengal Volunteers, which later became the most important centre of all revolutionary actions. He had moved from Dhaka to Midnapore and organised the boys, exhorting them to do and die for the country. Revolutionaries trained by him were responsible for the assassination of three District Magistrates in succession, Peddy, Douglas and Burge. Summoned by the leadership to Calcutta for a major action, he left Midnapore immediately, never to return.

The bullet that had lodged in Dinesh's throat was not extracted, to avoid death during an operation. He recuperated and faced a long trial. The doctors and nurses took good care of him. His endearing behaviour charmed all. A senior nurse once asked him why he had taken poison and shot himself. He replied that it was to kill himself after his mission was over. Upon being asked whether he hated all British people, he calmly replied that he hated only those who hated Indians and wanted to rule over his motherland. He was tried in a special tribunal headed by Session Judge R R Galik. After a long trial, Dinesh was sentenced to death by hanging. The entire country was aghast and shocked.

When a sergeant came to take away Dinesh from his

condemned cell to the gallows on 6 July 1931, Dinesh handed over a bunch of letters that he had written to his near and dear (sister) and requested him to despatch them. He took bath by himself, singing all the while.

'Are'nt you afraid of death young man?', queried the sergeant, amazed at his fearless behaviour.

'Fear?' laughed Dinesh. 'I am just changing my shell – the body. My soul shall take a new body. We may meet here again.'

The sergeant was dumbstruck. His stupor was broken as Dinesh laughed out loud and said, 'I am ready, Let's go'.

'Do you have anything to say', asked a magistrate present.

'Please stop', thundered Dinesh. 'You know pretty well who has taken our rights to say. What is the need of such formal questions then? Please do your duty.' Saying so, the brave soldier of freedom shouted, Vande Mataram, as he stood on the gallows, before being hanged. The entire jail resonated with Vande Mataram. The spectator crowd outside shouted, 'Shaeed Dinesh Zindabad'.

All the markets, offices, courts closed down for the day. People had a faint hope that due to enormous pressure from eminent persons, the sentence may get commuted. That was not to be.

The Midnapore branch of Bengal Volunteers pledged

revenge and killed Galik later.

The third member of the group was **Badal Gupta** alias Sudhir, also 20 years old, and a member of the Bengal Volunteers. His body was kept in the morgue as his identity was not established. A card was found on him which had B N Dey written on it. The police were not convinced. After extensive enquiry, the body was identified as that of one Sudhir Gupta. He came from a family of revolutionaries. He was one the most disciplined and obedient members of the group and executed his assigned missions adroitly, earning the respect of his seniors. His body was handed over to his family and he was cremated in the presence of thousands of mourners.

THE AGNIKANYAS

'Yesterday, at about eleven at night, the Assam-Bengal Railway European Club was attacked daringly by a group of so-called revolutionaries', said the English language newspapers.
'A lady in men's uniform was leading the group. The attack left one European lady dead and several others grievously injured. The lady attired in men's army uniform was found lying dead near the club.'

BY DECEMBER 1930, WHILE in hiding, news came to Masterda that J I Craig, Chittagong's notorious police chief, would be travelling to Chandpur. The decision to eliminate him was taken. Ramkrishna Biswas, the one who could not

Preetilata storming the European Club

take part in the armoury raid due to injuries he sustained during testing of bombs before the raid, volunteered to kill Craig, along with another activist, Kalipada Chakravarty.

They took a train to Chandpur and waited.

The moment the train entered the station, the two quickly boarded the first class compartment. There they saw a tall person with an overcoat and hat, matching Craig's description. Without wasting time, they shot the man at point blank range and ran out.

The dead man was not Craig. He was a railway inspector, Tarini Mukherji, who looked like Craig. Before dying, Tarini said, one of the assailants wore a blue shawl. A very strict vigil was set and soon Ramakrishna and Kalipada were apprehended, based on this information. They were carrying three loaded revolvers, bombs and cartridges.

Convicted after a swift trial, Ramakrishna was sentenced to be hanged while Kalipada was sentenced to life in the Andamans.

While Ramakrishna was awaiting death, a young girl declaring herself as Ramakrishna's younger sister, used to meet him in Alipore central jail. She, on behalf of the revolutionaries, carried and delivered information. She was Preetilata Waddedar, an epitome of organisational excellence, daring and commitment.

PREETILATA

Preetilata Waddedar was born to a middle-class family of Chittagong. She went to Dhaka for her Intermediate classes before moving to Calcutta for studying BA at the prestigious Bethune college. While in Dhaka, she came into contact with an underground revolutionary group. Later she joined Masterda's group despite stiff objections from some senior leaders. Her daring acts soon made her acceptable to them and she was known by her nickname 'Rani'.

The hanging of Ramakrishna Biswas and then the death of Nirmal Sen had made her resolve to get involved in a direct action and make the revenge more intense. This Joan of Arc from India remains in the annals of history as an example of sacrifice and bravery.

In June 1932, Surya Sen, Nirmal Sen, Apurba Sen and Preetilata Waddedar were hiding in an upper floor in the house of one Savitri Devi at Dhalaghat. Suddenly the house was encircled by a Gurkha brigade, led by one Captain Cameron. Surya Sen asked Preetilata to go downstairs and try to escape, and the men took up position on the first floor. Cameron, eager to capture Surya Sen, hurriedly climbed up the stairs only to be shot dead by Nirmal Sen. Intense firing followed. Nirmal Sen lay dead. After a while Surya Sen came down with Apurba Sen, revolvers in hand and somehow sneaked out with Preetilata. Running through the trees, Apurba Sen got shot in the chest and fell dead.

The newspapers next day carried the news of the encounter on the first page.

Running through a deluge, Surya Sen and Preetilata took shelter at the house of a man named Mahendra. For the first time, the lion-hearted Masterda (Surya Sen) had tears in his eyes. His right hand, Nirmal was no more. He was feeling his absence. The task of freeing the country seemed pushed back. Masterda was crestfallen.

The death of Captain Cameron agitated the administration. The prize money for capturing Surya Sen or giving information about him was raised. A lookout notices for Preetilata, aged 19, was also issued.

24 September 1932. A few days ago, an abortive attempt to plan and attack the European Club at Chittagong was made by the revolutionaries. Preetilata approached Masterda and requested him to let her lead one more attack on the club. Masterda was hesitant. He had by then lost most of his trusted men. He had, however, to yield before Preeti's insistence.

Dressed in full military outfit, Preeti took Masterda's blessings and parted ways. She told him that it might turn out to be her last meeting with Masterda.

At the appointed hour, Preetilata, along with her group of eight men, converged near the club. Two of them, disguised as coachmen, entered the premises, ostensibly to drink water. Preeti and the others sneaked in through the rear door stealthily. At that hour, the club activities were at its peak. Drinking and dancing were in progress. Around fifty Europeans were enjoying the night. All of a sudden, hell broke loose. The club resounded with bombs and pistol fire. Jalianwalah Bagh, where innocent Indians had lain dead, was being revenged. Preetilata and the others were paying back the British in the same coin.

'Company, fall in. Our job is over. Let's go back. Ready. Quick march', Preetilata gave the order. Running out, the group scattered in different direction. Armoured vehicles and military personnel had reached the club by then. Preetilata stayed back at the premises, to continue shooting, allowing her team to escape. Soon she was surrounded by the army. With no escape, she committed suicide by consuming cyanide. The others had made good their escape.

The woman found dead on the lawn was identified as Preetilata, daughter of Jagatbandhu Waddedar of Chittagong. A revolver and a few cartridges were found on her person. After enquiry, the body was handed over to her father. The first woman martyr of this fiery era was consigned to the flames but fearing the police, no one came to pay her the last respect. Just a day before, she had written an impassioned letter to her mother, urging her not to cry once she was dead as she had to die for her motherland.

KALPANA DUTTA

Following Masterda's arrest, the revolutionaries were restless. Kalpana Dutta was still absconding. Her family assets were attached by the administration. Tarkeshwar Datta and Kalpana Datta then hatched a plan to free Masterda from the jail. Some revolutionaries within the jail started developing a sympathisers' network, joined by some sepoys, wardens and jail officials. Within no time, duplicate keys, revolvers, bomb making chemicals were smuggled in. The plan failed at the last stage due to the arrest of a key conspirator.

A few days before Preetilata embarked upon the attack on the European Club at Pahartali in Chittagong, a similar attack on the club had been planned by the revolutionaries. A taxi carrying a few passengers had arrived near the club. The passengers alighted and went past the club several times. A police informer suspected something foul and tailed them. The man moved closer to the cab and discovered to his utmost surprise that one of the passengers was a female, dressed in male attire. He dutifully informed the police, who cordoned the area swiftly and apprehended the group. The female dressed in a male attire was the fiery Kalpana Dutta. She was released on bail as no crime was committed. She vanished soon after.

On the run, Kalpana Dutta, along with the new commander Tarkeshwar Dastidar and Manoranjan Das, took shelter in the house of one Purna Talukdar in Gahira village. Receiving information on their location, the police surrounded the safehouse. Finding it impossible to sneak out, the trio engaged in a fierce gunfight. The gunfight left the house owner and Manoranjan dead. Tarkeshwar and Kalpana Dutta were arrested.

Kalpana Dutta, born in 1913, was the daughter of a government employee in Chittagong. At the age of seventeen, she went to Calcutta and joined Bethune college. She was highly influenced by Khudiram Bose and Kanailal Datta. While in college, she came in touch with Surya Sen (Masterda), Ananta Singh and other noted revolutionaries. Initially hesitant to induct her, the leaders agreed to induct her due to her daring, commitment, endurance and the ability to don various disguises.

Kalpana Dutta underwent rigorous training under several noted trainers of guerrilla warfare. She could remain underwater, with a reed in her mouth to take in air for a considerable time. She, along with her friend Preetilata, did intense firing practice. She also learnt to make gun cotton, a dreaded explosive. While the leaders of her group were in prison, she carried explosives from Calcutta, made bombs and dynamites and planned to blow the prison to free the leaders. The plan went awry at the last moment. Kalpana Dutta was sentenced to transportation for life. She was released in 1939 at the behest of the great poet, Rabindranath Tagore.

She graduated from Calcutta university in 1940 and joined the Communist Party of India to serve the people of Chittagong. She came over to India from East Pakistan in 1947, and died in 1995. Kalpana married CPI leader P C Joshi and lived in Delhi in her last days.

BINA DAS

While Preetilata and Kalpana were directly connected to the group headed by the legendary Surya Sen after initiation with the Chattri Sangha, Bina Das was a long-standing member of Chattri Sangha. She too, like Preetilata and Kalpana, was a student at Bethune College, Calcutta. Bina's parents were prominent freedom fighters engaged in the upliftment of society as social workers in Bengal. Her father Beni Madhav Das had taught Netaji Subhas Chandra Bose and many other revolutionaries. Bina, since her young age, had a defiant streak. She wanted to free her motherland from the clutches of the British Empire and thought that armed revolution was the only way out.

During her school days, when the British Viceroy's wife was to visit the school, she pulled out of the team which was to scatter flowers at the Lady's feet, refusing to do so. This upset her teachers. The atrocities by the British pained her and stoked the fire of freedom in her. She became more resolute as she grew up. Bina Das organised the first protest of the Chattri Sangha, when they protested against the Simon Commission in 1928. As the girl students kept protesting under her leadership, the uncompromising British principal resigned.

Her moment of glory came soon. In February 1932, the Governor of Bengal, Stanley Jackson, was to be the guest of honour of the Calcutta University convocation. Bina had arranged a pistol from a fellow woman revolutionary. As the Governor climbed up the aisle, Bina pulled out the pistol and fired at him. However, in the excitement and for want of practice, the bullets missed their target. Stanley Jackson escaped unhurt as his wife watched in disbelief. Bina was overpowered. A pistol and few cartridges were found on her person. The country was aghast and stunned. The newspapers carried the news of the attack on the Governor on front pages and it was also prominently published abroad, providing a major fillip to the struggle for independence.

Even after intense grilling, she refused to name her co-conspirators. During her trials he said, 'I confess that I fired at the Governor on the Convocation Day at the Senate House. I hold myself entirely responsible for it. My object was to die and if I had to die, I wanted to do it nobly, fighting against this despotic system… I fired at the Governor, impelled by my love for my country which is being repressed'. Bina Das was sentenced to nine years of imprisonment.

Bina was nicknamed, Agnikanya (woman of fire). She was awarded a mere Padma Shri by the Government of India in 1960. Her B A (Hons) degree was awarded to her eight decades later, in 2012, posthumously. Such is the honour we bestowed on a brave daughter of India. She died in Rishikesh. Her unkempt body was found in a drain. She lay unclaimed till someone recognised her after a couple of days. The Agnikanya who left all pleasures of life to fight for her country, lived her life neglected by her countrymen, uncared for and forgotten.

THE HEROIC SAGA OF MIDNAPORE

It was a local school show. Midnapore's district magistrate James Peddy was looking intently at the paintings while the school children and their parents crowded the place. Darkness had set in and lanterns were lit for the show. Mingling with the crowd in failing lights, the two daredevils inched towards Peddy and pulling out their pistols, fired point blank at the official. Peddy shuddered and writhing in pain, slumped on a bench. The two young men had exhausted their bullets. Death was imminent. Temporarily dazed and overwhelmed at their success, they took seconds to recover before taking out the cyanide ampoules they carried.

Bimal Dasgupta and Jatijiban Ghosh shoot Peddy

> *Looking around they were surprised to see no one in the room. Everyone had fled, including Peddy's bodyguards.*
>
> *The two young assassins ran out, took a side path and within minutes, were out of the school compound.*

THE DEATH SENTENCE TO Dinesh Gupta in the Writers Building shootout had sent waves of sadness, despair and anger through the young revolutionaries of Midnapore. Gupta had set up a branch of the Bengal Volunteers in Midnapore town in 1927, in accordance with the directives of the central command. Here he had assiduously developed a formidable local group of young men as revolutionaries. The young men were in awe of his organisational acumen and loved his cheerful disposition too. They were totally dedicated to Dinesh and were ready to sacrifice their lives at his single command. It was natural that Midnapore's youth were particularly upset and promised revenge for Dinesh at the earliest.

Dinesh Gupta had been insisting on three basics of all covert battles – camouflage, honourable retreat and fixing of an opportune moment to strike. His group members feigned allegiance to the Congress party and professed a non-violent line of struggle. Covertly, they engaged in the policy of 'Eye for an eye, tooth for a tooth and blood for blood'. The orders for any armed operation came from the central command. The executors were screened and chosen by the central leadership, the time and place were notified later, and arms were supplied on time, through secure conduits. This was essential to maintain secrecy. The BV members of Midnapore were growing impatient; their slogan was, 'Death before Dishonour. Act and face death'.

Midnapore's District Magistrate James Peddy had been instrumental in ruthless suppression of anti-government protests, he even sanctioned torture of young school and college-going students and inculcated fear in the minds of ordinary citizens. He was infamous for atrocities on female revolutionaries, jailed on flimsy grounds, his methods included smearing chili powder in their private parts to extract confessions. The local BV team had decided to eliminate Peddy.

Accordingly, the central command sent arms and ammunitions to Kharagpur, to be collected by the Midnapore branch for the action. The arms reached safely to the Midnapore revolutionaries. In 1931, a strike at Peddy by two young boys, Bimal Dasgupta and Jatijiban Ghosh, had to be abandoned at the last moment, as Peddy had changed his plans to distribute awards to loyal staff and had on the appointed day left his office early. The failure disheartened the leadership and senior BV members came down to Midnapore to look for a moment to strike.

The moment came in April. On 1 April 1931, Peddy was to inaugurate an exhibition at the Midnapore collegiate school. Bimal and Jatijiban had been briefed to be as close to Peddy and fire simultaneously, avoiding civilian casualty. Unfortunately, again, Peddy had not turned up. The plan had to be aborted. It was risky to let the youngsters keep the arms. Finally, a day came, when he was to really visit the exhibition.

On 7 April, Peddy was due to inspect the school exhibition and distribute awards. Bimal and Jatijiban engaged themselves in a friendly football match opposite the District Magistrate's bungalow – all the while keeping an eye on the activities in the DM's house. When finally, Peddy moved out of his bungalow with his bodyguards and proceeded to the venue, Bimal and Jati rushed to their houses, changed into fresh clothes and tucked their pistols under their dresses. They executed the mission they were assigned flawlessly.

After the Peddy assault, the two teenagers decided to take a cycle and pedal away to Bankura. It was a rickety cycle and they had to change the plan. Leaving the cycle in a bush, they took a train to Purulia. Though it was a grave risk, they took it as they were confident that no one would expose them as Peddy was hated by all. From Purulia, they went to a safe house in Calcutta. The central committee members were ecstatic. Dinesh Gupta was still in jail waiting to be hanged. The news of Peddy's murder was a solace to him before death.

Peddy died the following day. The attackers were at large. Senior British police officials descended in Midnapore. There was no clue. No one came forward to depose they had seen anything, noticed anyone. Following a detailed investigation, they were told by a small boy that Peddy was killed by Bimal Dasgupta. Meanwhile, Bimal had come back to his home, confident that he had not been identified. With the turn of events, he was counselled to leave Midnapore. He hid in a library the next day and took a night train to Calcutta, in the guise of a milkman's son. His Bihari milkman took him to Calcutta at a grave risk. Bimal reached Calcutta safely and was moved to a safehouse in a colliery near Dhanbad.

On 7 July, Dinesh Gupta went to the gallows. His case was presided over by Magistrate Galik. To have a case in the court of Ralph Reynolds Galik meant the harshest punishment for the revolutionaries. He, as a president of Special Tribunal, gave the orders to hang Dinesh Gupta for the Writers building shootout.

The action squad of Bengal Volunteers then passed a

resolution to eliminate him. The killing was to be done on 18 July and Bimal was chosen to execute the killing. However, at the last moment, he was withdrawn from the action.

Galik was killed within twenty days of the verdict, however.

On 27 July, a meek-looking youth with a soiled shirt and dhuti was travelling to Alipore in a bus. He carried an umbrella. The umbrella had a loaded pistol. The young man was on a mission. A mission with the least chances of returning alive.

Before he embarked on the mission, his mentor, Sunil Chatterji, had asked him to write on a piece of paper, 'Vande Mataram. Get destroyed. Take the prize for injustice to Dinesh Gupta'. The note was signed, Bimal Gupta. He was then instructed to keep the chit in his right pocket and a cyanide capsule in the left pocket.

Peddy, another magistrate, had been shot dead by Bimal Dasgupta and Jatijiban Ghosh after a verdict from Peddy and the police were on lookout for them.

The young revolutionary had been trained by his mentor in a jungle and his name was yet not on the police blacklist. Meanwhile, Galik's security had been tightened. It was difficult to enter his courtroom and to come out of the room alive. Nevertheless, Galik's court was always crowded.

The young man, Kanai Lal Bhattacharya, managed to slip into the crowded room and moved close to the dais. Galik returned from lunch and took his seat. The crowd stood up in reverence. Chatterji, his mentor, saw Kanai reach the front row of spectators and rushed out to his waiting taxi and waited for Kanai to return after the act, if possible.

Minutes ticked by, Galik dug his head into the files. The court fell silent. Kanai kept looking at him. Then, remembering his Guru, Dinesh Gupta, Kanai took a deep breath, walked to the witness box and before anyone could react, fired at Galik. The bullet missed its mark and hit the ceiling. A seasoned gymnast, Kanai jumped on the heavy wooden railing of the witness box and fired again at Galik. This time the bullet found its mark and went through Galik's forehead. He slumped to his death instantly.

A policeman fired at Kanai. He missed and got a bullet from Kanai in his shoulders. By then, other policemen had begun to shoot at Kanai. He was hit in the abdomen, legs and fell down. Death was near. He bit the cyanide capsule. The detective department ran in to find the dead body with the chit. The chit said he was Bimal Gupta, the one who had killed Peddy a few days ago.

The body, however, did not match Bimal's description with the police. The body stayed unclaimed for long. Many days later, the police said, it was of Kanai Lal Bhattacharya from the 24 parganas.

The ruse to divert police attention from Bimal Gupta had failed. Kanai had written to his mother that he would come to see her soon. Instead, she heard her son had become a martyr.

After 1930, the European merchants became vocal and highly critical of the revolutionaries. *The Statesman* and *The Englishman* newspapers, controlled by them, wrote that the 'terrorists' had their leaders in jails wherefrom the revolution was being controlled. They opined that for each Englishman killed, a leader should be taken out and shot in broad daylight. Taking the cue from such articles, unwarranted police firing inside Hijli jail near Kharagpur resulted in two deaths and several injuries. The incident, unheard of in any country till that day, was received with anger and hatred all over.

The president of the European Association at that time was a man called E Villiers. The Bengal Volunteers decided to kill him for his anti-revolutionary stance which had resulted in the firing inside Hijli jail. Bimal Dasgupta was assigned the task of eliminating him. Bimal was very excited as he had got a 'Double Action' chance – a rare honour.

On 29 October 1931, dressed as a Muslim businessman, Bimal entered Gillander's House, an office building in

Calcutta, which had Villiers' office room. He waited for the signal that Villiers was in his office. He pretended to be smoking as a camouflage. The revolutionaries were forbidden to smoke, drink or engage in anti-social acts and he smoked, to evade police attention. After a while, the signal came.

Bimal rushed to Villiers' room and started firing. Villiers was supposed to be alone but at that moment, three or four Europeans were already present. Alerted by one of them, Villiers ducked under the table. The rest of the Europeans pounced on Bimal, who was firing from the door. He did not get time to consume cyanide. Asked about his motive, he said, 'listen, the savage repressions in Midnapore, Chittagong and the Hijli camp were always inspired by the European Association. I came to settle accounts with its president'.

Taken to the police headquarters, he was beaten up so badly that he nearly lost his sense. The brave boy still refused to divulge any names of his controllers. He burst into laughter while being taken to the jail. Enraged, the policemen kicked him repeatedly, asking him why he was laughing. Bimal later confided that he had laughed in satisfaction that the police were unable to extract any information from him.

The trial for the Villiers shooting started in November

1931. Villiers, the main witness, had by then left India for safer grounds – England. He knew that the revolutionaries would pursue him till he died. The case thus became weak, and Bimal was awarded a ten years' rigorous imprisonment. He had got off lightly as Subhas Bose had convinced the prosecution counsel not to insist on a harsher sentence, as the Peddy murder trial was also on, in which Bimal was destined to go to the gallows.

When the Peddy trial began, the police were not able to identify or capture the second killer Jatijiban. The witnesses were systematically and repeatedly fed with anti-British propaganda. As a result, the witnesses deposed in the negative, influenced by the talk or the fear of repercussions from the revolutionaries. Even the boy who had said that he had seen Bimal killing Peddy, retracted saying, 'though he knew Bimalda, he had not seen him shooting'. The case grew weaker and eventually, Bimal Dasgupta was acquitted of the charges.

This case was a big victory for the nationalists like Subhas Bose, his elder brother Sarat Bose and others. The British brought in a new rule that an attempt to murder or complicity in murder shall also attract death sentence.

The Hijli camp jail firing which had created a furore was investigated by a committee which did not attribute any 'lapse or excess' by the jail officers. As usual, a few sepoys on duty were indicted by it. The report was prepared by an infamous District Magistrate, Robert Douglas. It earned him a place in the blacklist of the revolutionaries.

The central command of Bengal Volunteers issued directions to the Midnapore cadre to kill Douglas at the earliest. Two of the boys, Prabhabshu Pal and Pramath Mukherji, were assigned the task of eliminating him. A third boy, Pradyote Bhattacharya, was kept as a standby as the stake was high.

Prabhanshu was from Midnapore but lived in Calcutta where his father was an eminent doctor. Prabhanshu was a well-built boy of cheerful disposition. Pradyote was from Midnapore too, where he studied at the Hindu school. He was a topper of his class. Both were summoned to the central command hideout in Kolkata. The leaders looked at Pradyote – he seemed so young but confident.

'Pradyote, till now we have not missed any target. You have to maintain that tradition. Will you be able to do it?', they asked.

'Of course.'

'Will you maintain secrecy if caught? There will be extreme torture, transportation with imprisonment for life, or death. Are you ready for death?'

'Of course,' replied the young tiger cub confidently.

'Then go back to Midnapore and wait for further

orders.' The leaders were convinced of his courage.

Soon there was information that Douglas was to cross River Kangsabati by an official boat. The boys were to wait at the ferry ghat, and fire at him from both sides. The revolvers had been delivered to them the previous day. Douglas came in, heavily guarded. There was no scope to go near him. Pramath Mukherji was impatiently shuffling and nervous. Prabhabshu took him along and left the place. Mukherji's nervousness was reported by a volunteer keeping watch on the action squad. A decision to replace him was taken. Pradoyte was brought in, in his place.

Days passed in anticipation of a strike, but Douglas was well guarded all the time. Then one day, Pradyote who used to visit the government offices for his scholarship, brought the news that Douglas was to head a board meeting on 31 March 1932 at the District Board office. A plan of the office was prepared, and action plan was made for an effective attack. The bodyguard was to be shot at first and Douglas was to be hit from two sides. A 450-bore revolver and a seven-chambered pistol were to be used. Douglas did not turn up on that day. The arms were shifted to a farmhouse for safety.

One of the BV leaders provided a typed message that read, 'a fitting reply to the premeditated, barbarous and cowardly attempt on the Patriotic Sons of Bengal – Bengal

Revolutionaries'. This was to be carried by the two boys. The wait continued.

Then came the news that the next Board meeting on 30 April was definitely to be chaired by Douglas. It was April again, a dreaded month on the BV calendar – after the Chittagong Arms raid and the Peddy killing, it was time to eliminate Douglas. The revolutionaries were upbeat. A new revolver was procured which was of .380 bore, with 23 bullets and of long range. It was tested one night for efficacy. However, reaching Douglas was not so easy. He rarely moved out without bodyguards. The meeting that he was to chair was to be attended by more than thirty senior officers, mostly armed, apart from their bodyguards. Many posters had sprouted in Midnapore promising action against the British and security in every office was tight.

On 30 April 1932, magistrate Douglas was in the chair. The Board meeting had started on time. Pradoyte and Prabhanshu lurked in the shadows outside. They had on light make up. While Prabhanshu had donned a thick moustache, Pradyote put on a pair of glassless spectacles. The boys tried to enter into the building's compound from a side gate but were accosted by a guard. The two had pretended to be Board employees and said, they had come to submit some important papers. The guards were adamant and refused entry. The same story was repeated at another gate. Time was running out. There was a barbed wire fence. The only way to get into the compound was by jumping over it. The two boys looked at each other and did the impossible. They jumped in and ran into the building; the guards were surprised, and it was too late to stop them. Pandemonium prevailed while the boys barged into the room where the meeting was on and fired at Douglas.

Unfortunately, Pradyote's revolver failed to fire while the one held by Prabhanshu fired at the target repeatedly. Douglas lay dead in a pool of blood. Douglas's guard had run out shouting, ostensibly to save himself. Pradyote stood firm, with the revolver pointed at the people in the room; they were too stunned and numb with fear to react. This provided Prabhanshu the chance to run out to safety. Prabhanshu ran, shooting randomly at his pursuers and vanished down a lane. He threw his false moustache away, on the way.

Moments later, Pradyote, waving his revolver, also ran out to a nearby school. He was pursued by the guards. As Pradyote took position inside the school, with his revolver pointed towards them, his pursuers stopped at the gate. They were unaware that the revolver was not working. Taking a chance, Pradyote ran to cross a wire fence when his dhoti got entangled in the barbs. By the time he extricated himself, a stone struck him on his forehead, and he fell down. A hefty bodyguard pounced at him and rained kicks and blows on him. He was just a frail young boy.

Taken to jail, he said he was tired and wanted to bathe and sleep. His wish was granted. The police could not elicit any information about anyone from him even after inhuman torture. The brave boy endured it stoically. The intelligence team interrogating him asked him why, even though he was a bright and diligent student, he was carrying a revolver which failed him at the crucial time. Touching his forehead with his handcuffed hands, he replied, 'Irony of fate Sir. Had my revolver spoken, I would not have been here in this condition. The story would have been different....'

He was tried for murder, conspiracy, and abetment by a special tribunal. He was sentenced to death on 26 June. His mother appealed, much against his wishes, but the sentence remained the same.

On 12 January 1933, at 6 o'clock in the morning, this fearless son of mother India stood poised before the rope hanging for him. The new District Magistrate, Bernard E J Burge, was present at Pradyote's hanging. He asked, 'Are you ready Pradyote?'

'One minute please, Mr Burge, I have something to say', Pradyote replied.

'Yes, speak out, I am listening', said Burge.

'We are determined, Mr Burge, not to allow any European to remain in Midnapore. Yours is the next turn, get yourself ready…. I am not afraid of death. Each drop of my blood will give birth to hundreds of Pradyotes in all the houses of Bengal. Yes. Do your work please.' Saying so, the young Bengal tiger bade farewell to his loved motherland.

Prabhanshu remained unidentified and untraceable. He lived on to see his country attain freedom and to satisfactorily recount his accomplishment.

The three consecutive killings of officials had terrified the British administration in Midnapore. No one wanted to become a DM. Finally, Bernard Burge said yes to the post. He, however, was extremely cunning and cautious, and never stirred out of his home. Yet, Pradyote's warning was not to be taken lightly. The BV decided to eliminate Burge in the dreaded month of April – the month of revenge. A core team of hardcore young revolutionaries was formed for action, but a sudden raid on BV safehouses led to a spurt of arrests of their many senior leaders. So, the group waited for the next good chance to kill Burge.

The time came on 2 September 1933. As vengeful April had passed without any attack, Burge and the police force relaxed their guard. Midnapore lived under heavy police presence. This was when a football match between two local clubs was organised, to be played at the police grounds. Senior officials, including Burge, were to play for the clubs. And Burge was a keen footballer. The ground housed the police armoury on one side and the jail on the other.

The Bengal Volunteers decided that Burge would be eliminated on the field, in the presence of his police force. It was a suicidal mission but there was a beeline of revolutionaries ready to do the honours.

The task fell on Anath Panja and Mrigen Datta, two young men in their early twenties.

Five o'clock in the evening. The match was about to start. Senior police officials like Linton, Jones, Smith were already there. With great stealth, Anath and Mrigen sneaked into the milling crowd ready to watch the match. Burge alighted from his car and proceeded to the field. Suddenly, AnathPanja and Mrigen Datta appeared from nowhere and shot Burge fatally. The shots caused a stampede, and the police officers ran here and there. Jones, a police officer, got a shot in his leg and fell down.

Burge had slumped to the ground, severely injured and profusely bleeding. Pradyote's face must have come to his mind while passing out. In a frenzy, Anath Panja sat on his fallen body and pumped a few more bullets in his body. By then, the police had recovered from their initial shock, and in a hail of return fire, Anath Panja and Mrigen Datta were killed.

England was shocked. Four senior officials were killed in three consecutive years 1931, 1932 and 1933. Entire India saluted the Midnapore Tigers. The frustrated administration, red faced, decided to teach Midnapore town a lesson. All suspected supporters, sympathisers and young men were rounded up, thrown in jail, tortured to elicit information about the conspirators. Their houses were burnt, properties were confiscated. People left Midnapore for safer places. The town wore a deserted look, with only the sound of heavy police boots on their way to raids. The atrocities were unparalleled. The savage side of the British – which boasted of 'Justice' came to the fore. Eventually, a trial commenced against a dozen suspected conspirators. No concrete evidence was found.

The Defence counsels were confident that they could get the accused released as none of the men on trial were in Midnapore at the time of the Burge killing. The unjust sentence jolted the country. Three of the accused, Nirmal Ghosh, Ramakrishna Roy and Brajakishore Chakravarty were sentenced to death and the rest were transported for life to the jail in Andaman. Englishmen again proved that their justice was really blind. The repeated killings jolted the British so much that Midnapore began to be administered from Calcutta.

In the year 1934, Sir John Anderson, a veteran of

anti-IRA administration took over as the Governor of Bengal. He had earned accolades for his actions in Ireland – a ruthless man. His Majesty's Government considered Anderson as the best suited person to suppress Bengal and its revolutionaries. The Bengal Volunteers took up the challenge to nullify Anderson. Though hugely outnumbered, their organisational prowess, secrecy, commitment to the cause made them a formidable force to reckon with. The European-controlled newspapers were emboldened by Anderson's appointment. 'No truck with the terrorists. Give the dog a bad name to hang him. If another European is murdered, detainees should be shot.' This, unfortunately, was echoed by some Indian leaders.

Practicing the tried and tested British policy of Divide and Rule, Anderson alienated the Muslim population of united Bengal by offering them bribes for spying and acting as informers. These people were small shopkeepers, traders and petty farmers. Cracks began to appear in Bengal's united religious fabric. Bengal Volunteers then decided that Anderson needed to be taught a lesson. It was to be firmly establish that the revolution was very much there and alive in Bengal.

The target this time was the Governor of Bengal, and the action contemplated was risky. The Governor was always in the high-security framework and mostly inaccessible.

In May, Anderson moved with his office to Darjeeling – a beautiful summer resort in the eastern Himalayas. He was followed by four revolutionaries. Ujjwala Majumdar and Manoranjan Banerjee – who pretended to be siblings and came in from Dhaka via Calcutta to the hill town. Bhabani Bhattacharya and Rabi Banerjee came directly from Dhaka. Ujjwala carried a harmonium which concealed the arms.

The opportunity arrived on 8 May. Anderson was to distribute prizes for the horse race to be held at the Lebong racecourse. Bhabani and Rabi entered the course after buying legitimate tickets for the races. Manoranjan and Ujjwala had gone away to Siliguri, to return to base after delivering the arms. The racecourse buzzed with policemen in plain clothes, spies and army men. Bhabani and Rabi sat a little away from the podium where Anderson sat. After the race, the Governor rose from his seat. Bhabani and Rabi were not able to move forward due to the police cordon and the occupied seats on the way, without raising suspicion. They aimed and fired from their positions. When the shots rang out, there was panic and confusion among the spectators. People ducked, ran without an inkling of what had happened. Bhabani's shots had missed the target. The ADC of the Governor fired four shots at him, grievously injuring Bhabani, who slumped in the stands. Rabi targeted Anderson, who was hit on his lips. He instantly hid behind his steno. The unfortunate lady received a shot while shielding her boss. One European sergeant was also shot. Meanwhile, a few bodyguards jumped on Rabi and overpowered him. He was beaten to pulp, rendering him immobile for life. Bhabani and Rabi were taken to the hospital. Regaining consciousness after a while, the first question Bhabani asked was, 'Is Anderson alive?' Anderson was very much alive but the sheer audacity of the attack rattled the empire. It was not considered a failure of the revolutionaries. It was a tactical and moral victory. The world now knew that the British are vulnerable in front of a committed organisation which held supremacy, due to the sheer bravery and sense of purpose of its committed members.

Manoranjan and Ujjwala – disguised as brother and sister – had reached Calcutta, evading the police. They were subsequently captured from a safehouse within days, along with many others suspected of collaborating. Seven of them were ultimately tried for the attempt to murder. Bhabani, during his trial, thundered, 'I came to assassinate the Governor. My object was to murder him. I have nothing more to say. No one but myself and Rabi took part in the action'. Rabi was paralysed by then for life due to the beating he had received. He tried to smile and nodded his head in agreement.

Bhabani and Rabi were handed death sentence.

Manoranjan Banerjee too was sentenced to death by hanging. Ujjwala Majumdar was sentenced to twenty years of deportation with rigorous imprisonment. Three others were given deportation orders, with varying years of imprisonment.

Under an appeal by a missionary school where Rabi studied, his sentence was commuted, and he was sent to England for rehabilitation. He was a brilliant student. The sentence of Manoranjan was also commuted to deportation and imprisonment for life. The Midnapore saga ended thus in a manner which shook the very foundations of the British empire.

There is no mention of the bravery, daring and sacrifice exhibited by the young boys from Midnapore in modern India's history books.

TARGET TEGART THE TERRIBLE

The statement given in a packed court, by a Ninth grade 17-year-old schoolboy, Gopinath Saha, stunned the country. Charles Tegart was in the court during the hearing. Gopinath said, 'I wanted to kill that tyrant, Tegart. I knew him, as I watched his movements for many hours. Alas, due to the mist and my excitement, I shot an innocent British man. I am extremely sad about that. But I am sadder to have missed the chance to finish this hated enemy of my country. I shall go with the hope that someday, someone will finish him. The country is full of patriots'.

Charles Tegart

CHARLES TEGART, AN IRISH police officer, had joined the Calcutta police in 1901. He became head of the Detective Department soon and set up an elaborate spy and informer network all over undivided Bengal. He was particularly harsh to the freedom fighters. Notorious for his uncompromising and brutal treatment of political detainees, he became one of the most hated police officers in Raj India. He was very efficient and ruthless. He was always on the move all the time, tracking the revolutionaries with dogged determination. He became the Commissioner of Police in 1927, holding the post till 1931. If there was one policeman the revolutionaries were awry of, it was Tegart. He used religious divides, family discord and brutality to elicit information. It was, therefore, natural that he was on the hit list of the revolutionaries for years. About six attempts were made to kill him. All of them failed, much to Tegart's delight. He continued to drive through the land in an open-roof car with his pet dog on the bonnet, showing off his invincibility. Later, he even wrote a book on his India days.

Two major attempts, one in 1924 by Gopinath Saha, and the other in 1934 by Dinesh Majumdar and Anuja Sengupta are worth recalling.

By 1923, Tegart had become a terror arresting people on trivial grounds, mounting combing operations and acting as a government greyhound, sniffing rebellion. The underground resistance was shaken. They resolved to kill Tegart, the terrible.

Gopinath Saha, a student of class Nine at Serampore near Calcutta, stayed with his elder brother. His mind was full of dreams — to free his motherland from the British. He did not want to live as a slave in his own country. Influenced by the revolutionaries, he met some of the movement workers and from them heard about Tegart. Saha felt that Tegart was a serious impediment in achieving freedom. He took it upon himself to kill Tegart. He managed to procure a pistol, and tucking it in his shirt, he roamed the possible places Tegart went to, in Calcutta. On 19 January, he saw Tegart near a shop front. Wasting no time, he pumped a few bullets at him.

It was unfortunately not Tegart. The victim was a look alike with a similar gait as that of Tegart. Ernst Day was an employee of Kilburn & Company. Out on his habitual morning stroll, he had paused before a shop. Gopinath, taking him to be Tegart, had fired at him.

Clutching his pistol, Gopinath ran through Park Street. He was followed by a Sikh taxi driver. Gopinath shot him in the abdomen. The driver lay injured in a pool of blood. Gopinath hailed a car which did not stop. Gopinath shot that driver too. By this time, a few policemen had converged at the place and as an European grappled with Gopinath, they overpowered Gopinath and neutralised him. Upon search, a Mauser pistol and a few cartridges were found on his person.

Ernst Day died the next day. With his death, the entire British population in the city cried for justice and severe punishment.

Gopinath's trial started soon after, where a young man stood in the courtroom repenting his inadvertent killing of an innocent person.

The trial went to the High court and as expected, the verdict was 'To be hanged till death'. On 1 March 1924, a young Gopinath Saha smilingly went to the gallows.

Subhas Chandra Bose and some other leaders waited outside the jail. Gopinath's body was not given to them. A handful of relatives were allowed in to perform the last rites within the jail premises. Even the ashes were not given to the family by the authorities.

Gopinath's sacrifice created a furore in Congress and a schism appeared. Mahatma Gandhi denounced his act though acknowledging Gopinath's love for the motherland. Deshbandhu Chittaranjan Das did not subscribe to this and passed an amendment praising Gopinath. Tegart was just lucky to escape this bid on his life and continued to hunt revolutionaries.

Year 1930. About 11 am in the morning on 25 August 1930, a car was parked in the crowded Dalhousie Square in Calcutta. There were three people in that car. Dinesh Majumdar, Anuja Sengupta and one more revolutionary, waiting with loaded revolvers and bombs. There was prior information that Tegart was to pass in his car, through the place. The minutes ticked by, and tension mounted. At last, Tegart's vehicle approached, and the occupants of the waiting car jumped out. Dinesh Majumdar threw a bomb which burst at the door of his vehicle but missed Tegart.

Anuja was a trifle late and his bomb exploded in his own hands, exposing his innards. He crawled to a park railing, trying to remain straight and fired from his pistol but collapsed to death soon. Dinesh tried to run away through the shocked crowd, severely injured. He lost his senses and fell on the pavement. The third revolutionary managed to escape and was never to be caught.

Tegart was lucky once again. He escaped unhurt. It was noted that the revolvers that Dinesh and Anuja had were from the Chittagong armoury. Tegart arrested all the men connected to the attack. Ten people were tried for treason and attempted murder. Eight of them were sentenced to transportation with imprisonment up to twenty years each. A special tribunal sentenced Dinesh to life imprisonment in the Cellular jail. He was initially kept in the Midnapore jail. After two years he jumped the high walls of the prison and fled.

Arrested after a while, he was sentenced to death and sent to gallows in June 1934.

Tegart by then had left India. He was bestowed with Knighthood and was entrusted with countering the Arabs in the Middle East, where he earned name and fame. Tegart, post retirement, kept a defused bomb on his table as a reminder to the threats to his life.

Obviously, Britain still thought it could and would hold its colonies in the Middle East and India.

THE FLAG MUST FLY

A crowd of nearly 8,000 hungry people were marching towards the main police station of Tamluk town on 29 September 1942. Firing soon started to stop the advancing crowd and the streets of Tamluk were drenched in blood. One Ramchandra Bera, shot in the chest, crawled close to the police station and shouted that he had reached his target. A rush of protestors followed him. From one side rushed in a 73-year old woman, an Indian flag in hand, leading thousands of protestors. The woman was Matangini Hazra, known to all as Gandhi Buri (old lady Gandhi) — an ardent follower of Mahatma Gandhi for years.

Matangini marches forward with the Indian Flag

The police warned her not to proceed further as section 144 was in force. Hazra pressed on, imploring the native policemen to leave the services of their colonial master and join the protest. Hazra was shot in both hands. Blood dripping from her wounded hands, she did not lose her grip on the flag and marched forward. This time a bullet hit her on her forehead. Matangini Hazra died instantly amidst cries of Quit India and Vande Mataram.

IN 1942, THE QUIT INDIA movement engulfed India. There were protests all over. Calcutta, Midnapore, Satara in Maharashtra, Ballia in United Provinces and Bhagalpur in Bihar. British rule was nearly over in many of these places. 1942-43 were also years of acute food shortage in Bengal (known later as the great Bengal famine); the British, engaged in World War II, used all the rice grown in Bengal to feed their troops all over the world. As a result, more than five million people were starving and there were protests against the colonial dispensation throughout the country.

Midnapore, in particular, was a hotspot of revolution and armed struggle and was in the forefront of protests. Kanthi and Tamluk towns of the district were engulfed in rebellion. For the British, Midnapore was dangerous. Intelligence reports had indicated that the Japanese were planning an invasion via the seas to join with the rebels of India. Waterways were to be used for fast movement. The British got into action. They banned use of boats and cycles across united Bengal and Assam and burnt them if they were found to be in use. Grain movement was brought to a complete halt. Laws were brought in against small farmers for stocking food grains. At the same time, hundreds of tonnes of rice were sent to the British forces elsewhere. The district faced huge deficit of rice – the staple food of local people.

In September, 3,000 people had tried to resist the export of rice from a rice mill near Midnapore. The police had fired at the unarmed gathering. Two villagers lay dead, and hundreds were injured. The faceoff infuriated the populace and the Quit India movement gained momentum. In Tamluk, people came out in the streets and gheraoed the police posts. War was declared against the government. Government offices were boycotted, and tax payments were stopped. The administration responded with iron hands. In late September, thousands of Hindus and Muslims cut off government communication lines, demolished bridges and blocked roads.

Matangini Hazra was born near Tamluk town in Midnapore, Bengal in 1870, in a poor family. She could not even get primary education and was married off early.

She was widowed at the age of 18 and had no children. She came back to her maternal home and began doing social service. Highly influenced by the Gandhian philosophy, she became an ardent follower of the Mahatma. By 1905, she was fully into the Independence movement and took part in civil disobedience movements and other non-violent protests.

By 1930, Midnapore was one of British India's most turbulent districts, a district resisting the British in both violent and non-violent ways. Women were in the forefront of agitations and Matangini was one of the most active leaders. In 1932, she vigorously took part in the Salt Satyagraha and led others to civil disobedience. She was arrested for breaking the Salt Act. The frail 62-year old was made to walk miles barefoot as a punishment. Matangini later participated in the movement to abolish Chowkidari tax and was arrested again and awarded a six month prison sentence.

After her release, she joined the Indian National Congress. She spun khadi (cotton fabric made by hand) on her own charkha (spinning wheel) and wore her self-made saris. During a severe outbreak of smallpox, she nursed the sick day and night, caring little for her own self.

The Governor of Bengal, Sir John Anderson, visited Tamluk in 1933 to address a public gathering. There was a huge police presence. Matangini dodged the police and reached the dais from where Anderson was speaking and waved a black flag. For her audacious and outrageous act, she was arrested on the spot and later sentenced to another six months of rigorous imprisonment.

In 1942, the British Indian government was ready for the Gandhi Buri, with British and Gorkha soldiers manning the main points in this suburban Bengal town. Matangini walked into the annals of history holding the Indian flag high. She was the oldest martyr in the history of India's freedom struggle.

After independence, her statues were put up in Tamluk and Calcutta, as a mark of respect. She remains unknown to people beyond Bengal.

Epilogue

The grandest revolutionaries I have met are the Bengal brand. In sheer excellence of character, they surpass their counterparts in any other country.

Sir Charles Tegart
British India's Commissioner of Bengal Police.

The stories of courage and sacrifice recounted in the pages of this book are only a few outstanding ones. There are hundreds more to be told. Documents like letters from the revolutionaries, jail records, police records are still available to substantiate the tales of daring, the revolutionaries' many brushes with the brutal colonial police force and the harsh punishment the young and old fighters received.

The actions may look easy now to read. One has to travel back to a time when there were no effective means of communication, severe punishment for anti-government acts and dearth of weapons to fight.

The words of the much feared, and one of the most competent police officers serving Calcutta Police for thirty long years, Charles Tegart, reflects the fear and admiration that the British had during the Agni Yug (Era of Fire) in Bengal. From 1900 to 1935 was this fiery era in Bengal, when disciplined and dedicated young men and women fought with the British army and police, with scarce resources in their hands but determination in their minds.

Annexing the Mughal Empire in 1857, the British retained their headquarters in Calcutta until 1912. Undivided Bengal was a gold mine with its natural resources, intelligent populace, and an easy access to the sea. Therefore, people of Bengal suffered the most in the hands of the British, who savoured the taste of victory for fifty years by enslaving a country.

By start of 1900, however, the people of Bengal grew restless for freedom. They felt only armed revolution could bring about their freedom. Under the guise of gymnasiums and citizens' aid committees, covert preparations for an armed revolution began. Young, healthy and serious-minded youths were picked up by mentors and groomed for actions against the British.

Anushilan Samiti led by Sarala Devi and Satish Chandra Bose was one of them. There was another group under Hemchandra Ghosh which later merged with the Bengal Volunteers, formed by Netaji Subhas Bose. Later, one group called Atmonnati group came up. These groups had presence in Dhaka, Chittagong and Midnapore with hundreds of branches all over Bengal.

A major group emerged with Aurobindo Ghosh and his brother Barin Ghosh under the name Jugantar. All these groups carried out actions like looting money to buy arms and engaged in sporadic skirmishes with the police. Then happened the Kingsford murder attempt which shook the British, followed by the famous Alipore Bomb-making Case. All these groups, in effect, terrorised the British and by 1912, they had moved the Raj capital to Mughal Delhi. Calcutta, however, continued to be a major commercial hub.

Soon, Gandhiji's non-violent struggle to attain freedom was being rendered irrelevant by Bengal's acts of daring violence. He was also acutely aware that the youth power of Bengal was a force to reckon with and, a Congressman of Subhas Bose's stature was among these hot-headed youth. Gandhi was, therefore, eager to bring these young men to his path of non-violence. He held many meetings with the senior leaders who covertly helped the armed revolution like Deshbandhu Chittaranjan Das, Subhas Chandra Bose, Sarat Bose, Jatindramohan Sengupta. He assured these leaders that he would get freedom by his non-violent means by 1925 or so. The men agreed and lay low. They joined the Indian National Congress and waited for Gandhiji's success. Nothing happened. The youth got restless. Subhas was the most restless. In 1928, during the Congress meet in Calcutta under the presidentship of Motilal Nehru, Subhas Bose arranged a long procession of men and women in military outfit. The group was later named as Bengal Volunteers.

Most of the spectacular strikes came from this group.

The most audacious strikes on the British started when the Bengali youth felt that now there was no other way than armed revolution, like the ones that happened earlier at Balasore. There was no respite for the British after 1928 in Bengal.

The revolutionaries of Bengal were highly trained, disciplined, dedicated and ready to sacrifice their lives to get their motherland freed. They were highly secretive. Their oath of not divulging any detail upon capture despite extreme torture stood firm. They obeyed the orders from their mentors or team leaders to the word, never questioning or raising queries.

The groups like Bengal Volunteers or BV and the

Chittagong Liberation Army had rank systems like professional national armed forces – General, Brigadier, Colonel etc., giving the members a sense of responsibility. This helped the strike force in the field.

The groups in general had two wings. One was to mobilise support and finance, and the other for overt and covert operations. The first group enrolled new volunteers, trained them in group ideals and imparted body and mind building trainings. The entrants to the group had to study, along with their course books, books about the revolutions in the different countries of the world like in France, Turkey, Ireland, Russia. They studied Giuseppe Mazzini, Kamal Pasha, Garibaldi, Lenin and got indoctrinated. Books by Swami Vivekananda, Bankim Chattopadhaya (*Ananda Math*), Ramesh Dutta, Tilak, Lajpat Rai and Gandhiji were widely read for character building. The *Bhagwat Gita* was the most read and followed book which gave solace to the young men. They intensively read newspapers to keep abreast of the changing political situation.

The second wing was involved in direct actions. They had to go by the secret oath and adherence to time. Nothing could come out of them. Only the ones who opted for death were chosen. The weak hearts had no place in this wing. The mission assigned depended on the temperament of the individual and the complexity of the mission.

There is no doubt that the secret organisations did a tremendous job of grooming selfless young men and women who laid down their lives without flinching an eyelid. However, there were hundreds of faceless individuals who helped the operations by acting as arms couriers, providers of safe houses and providers of logistics support.

A network of spies and informants kept the British in India. Under such conditions, often betrayed and cornered, highly committed groups carried on waves of assault on a much superior enemy. This was possible due to the courage of hundreds of unnamed men and women who lent support overtly or covertly, to the cause of India's freedom, putting their lives and properties at stake. They deserve our greatest respect. They suffered in silence as the British tortured them to elicit information, if caught. Many lost their homes, families, sanity and livelihood. Many died in jails. We should be grateful to them as long as our flag flies high.

All that the present generation can do is to accord them their rightful honour, going beyond all political biases.

JAI HIND

References

1. *Bidrohi Bharat* by Dr Niharranjan Sen (three volumes)

2. *Ami Subhas Bolchi* by Sailesh Dey (two volumes)

3. *Binoy-Badal-Dinesh* by Sailesh Dey

4. *Chittagong Armoury Raid* by Subodh Roy (one of the youngest members of the Jalalabad battle)

5. *Rakter Akshare* by Sailesh Dey

6. *Rodda Arms Loot* by Anand Chattopadhyay

7. Personal papers by British officers, and various Indian sources, magazines, blogs and cross references

8. Pics sources: Rightful owners

Picture Gallery (In sequence of episodes)

Durga Bhabhi with Family

Khudiram Bose

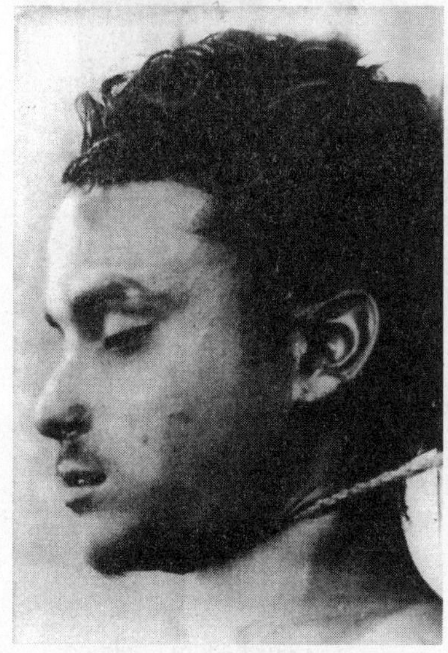

Prafulla Chaki

Kanailal Datta

Satyendra Nath Bose

Aurobindo Ghosh

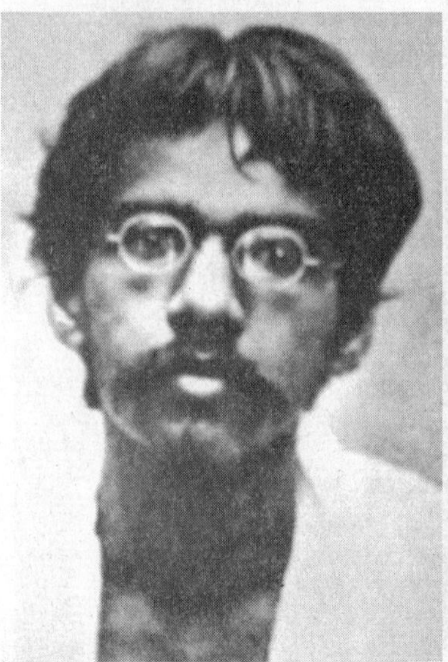

Barindra Kumar Ghosh

Hemchandra Kanungo

Ullaskar Datta

Satish Chandra Basu

Sarala Devi

Srish Chandra Pal

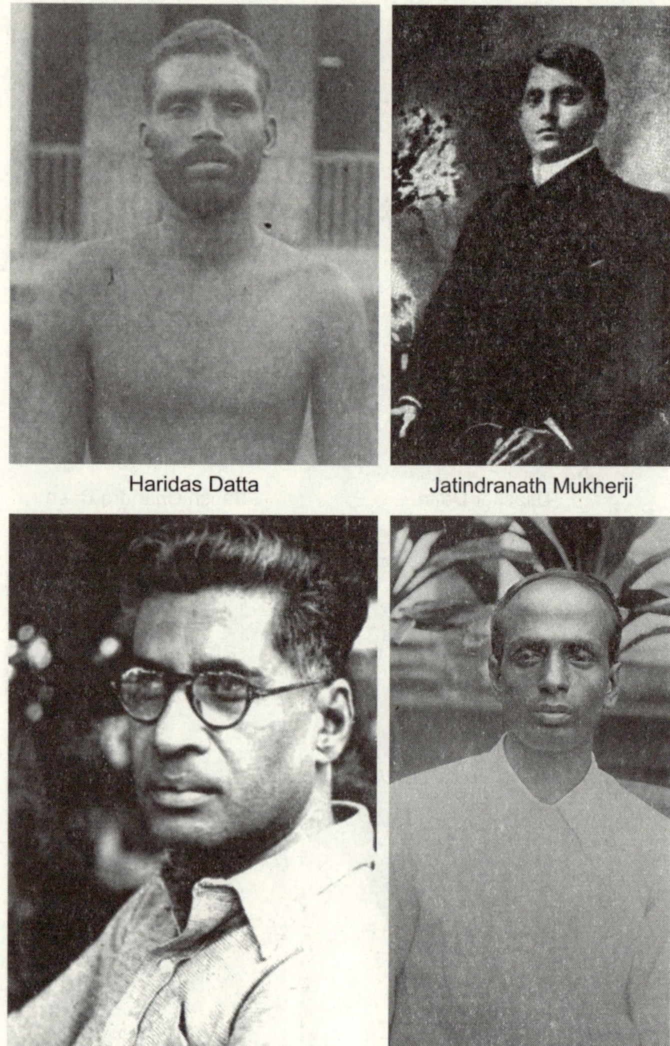

| Haridas Datta | Jatindranath Mukherji |
| M N Roy | Surya Sen |

Lokenath Bal

Ananta Singh

Ambika Chakrabarty

Ganesh Ghosh

Nirmal Sen

Subodh Roy

Benoy Basu

Badal Gupta

Dinesh Gupta

Preetilata Waddedar

Kalpana Dutt

Bina Das

Ramkrishna Biswas

Tarkeshwar Dastidar

Kanai Lal Bhattacharya

Pradyot Bhattacharya

Anath Bandhu Panja

Bhabani Bhattachary

Ujawala Majumdar

Manoranjan Banerji

Gopinath Saha

Dinesh Majumdar

Anuja Sengupta

Matangini Hazra

Bagha Jatin with mother, wife
and kids 1925

The place where Surya Sen was
hanged with Tarkeshwar Dastidar

Chittagong raid in papers

Jalalabad hills

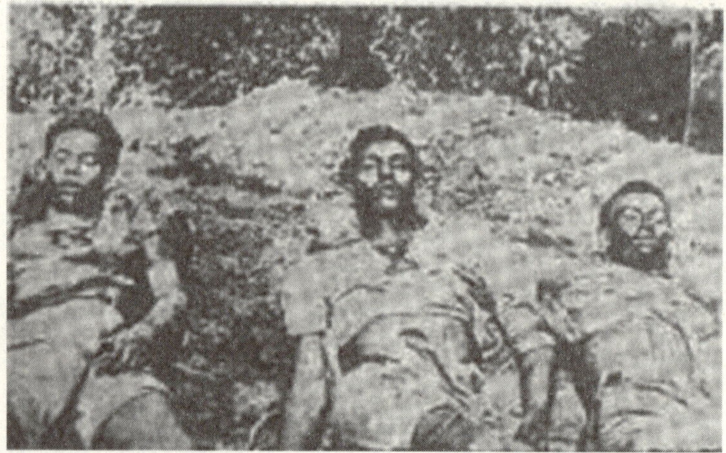

Some Martyrs of Jalalabad hills battle